Unequal Desires

Unequal Desires

Race and Erotic Capital in the Stripping Industry

SIOBHAN BROOKS

Author photograph (back cover): Beth Currans, photographer.

Frontispiece photograph: Karen Marisa, photographer; Teresa Ellis, model.

Published by State University of New York Press, Albany

© 2010 State University of New York

All rights reserved

Printed in the United States of America

No part of this book may be used or reproduced in any manner whatsoever
without written permission. No part of this book may be stored in a retrieval
system or transmitted in any form or by any means including electronic,
electrostatic, magnetic tape, mechanical, photocopying, recording, or otherwise
without the prior permission in writing of the publisher.

For information, contact State University of New York Press, Albany, NY
www.sunypress.edu

Production by Eileen Meehan
Marketing by Michael Campochiaro

Library of Congress Cataloging-in-Publication Data

Brooks, Siobhan, 1972–
    Unequal desires : race and erotic capital in the stripping industry /
Siobhan Brooks.
        p. cm.
    Includes bibliographical references and index.
    ISBN 978-1-4384-3215-1 (hardcover : alk. paper)
    ISBN 978-1-4384-3214-4 (pbk. : alk. paper)
    1. Sex-oriented businesses—History.   2. Race discrimination.   I. Title.

HQ115.B75 2010
306.77089'00917521—dc22   2009054441

10 9 8 7 6 5 4 3 2 1

I dedicate this book in memory of my mother, Aldean Brooks, for her belief in my intellectual abilities and unconditional love, and to sex workers of color.

Contents

Acknowledgments   ix

Introduction   1

1   A History of Desire Industries in New York City:
Burlesque, the Public Sphere, and the Construction of Morality   11

2   Marketing Desire and Geographic Coding in the Bronx   21

3   Race, Exchange, and Cultural Capital   37

4   Same-Sex Desire: Race, Class, and Gender Performance   49

5   Reproducing Cyber Desire: The Role of Technology and
Desire Industries   71

6   Labor Stratification in Desire Industries: Colorism,
Citizenship, and Erotic Capital   87

7   Conclusion: Race Versus Taste: Symbolic Racism in the
Post-Civil Rights Era   99

Appendix   103

Notes   107

References   115

Index   121

Acknowledgments

I thank my interviewees, whose insights and sharing of experiences made this book possible. I am very grateful for the feminist scholars of color whose work has guided me over the years, especially within the fields of queer studies, ethnic studies, and sociology. I received institutional support from the Department of Feminists Studies at University of California at Santa Barbara and the Gender Studies Department at Lawrence University during the completion of this project, which was based on my dissertation at New School University in the Sociology Department. I also thank Cathy Cohen and Juan Battle, organizers of the April 2008 conference, "Race, Sex, Power: New Movements in Black & Latina/o Sexualities," held at University of Illinois at Chicago, for allowing me to share my research with a broader audience. I am indebted to France Winddance Twine, who over the years has mentored me as a scholar, and I am grateful for our friendship during the past 12 years. I also thank Leila Rupp and Joane Nagel for their comments on earlier versions of the project.

I acknowledge the following people for offering me intellectual and emotional guidance throughout my research: Paul Amar, Eddy F. Alvarez, Youlanda Barber, Joan Budesa, Grace Chang, Lisa Hajjar, Zosera Kirkland, Robert Quintana Hopkins, Zakiyyah Jackson, Bahia Munem, Alice Matiz, Donna Marie Peters, Vanessa Rodriguez, Demetrius Semien, Charles Allen Swift Jr., and Mireille Miller-Young. I am also thankful to Larin McLaughlin, acquisitions editor at SUNY Press for all her support.

Finally, I thank my beloved partner, Alejandra Luna. I am deeply grateful for her love, for listening to me during my times of frustration and joy, and for always making me smile with her laughter. *Gracias por tu amor y apoyo. Te amo.*

Siobhan Brooks

Introduction

You have to try harder to talk to the customers and ease them into buying a lap dance from you, smile at them, engage them more, because many White men are scared of Black women and sometimes Black men don't want to see a Black woman either, whereas the White women have an easier time talking to customers. Some nights I make anywhere from $150 to $300 a night, whereas White women make around $500 a night or more.

—Alicia (24-year-old Black Canadian dancer)

On August 30, 1997, dancers at the Lusty Lady Theater in San Francisco made history by unionizing with Service Employees International Union (SEIU) Local 790; the Lusty Lady became the only strip club in the United States to successfully unionize (see Brooks, 1999). I was one of those dancers. When I was 22 years old I worked as an exotic dancer at the club while majoring in women's studies at San Francisco State University. Before working at the Lusty Lady, I was familiar with the sex workers movement in the Bay Area; in 1973 Margo St. James founded the prostitutes' rights group, COYOTE (Cast Off Your Old Tired Ethics), which fought to recognize sex work as labor, and eliminate the social stigma against sex workers. In the early 1990s, the movement was again in full force because of the influx of many women entering the sex industry, especially exotic dancing, as the service sector expanded. For example, in 1992, former exotic dancers Dawn Passar and Johanna Breyer founded the nonprofit organization the Exotic Dancers Alliance, and organized in response to a move by management forcing exotic dancers to pay stage fees to work in clubs.

I was familiar with the Lusty Lady because many of the students in my women's studies classes (most of whom were White) were working there; it was known as a feminist strip club because women managed it and the president of the company that owned it was a woman. Like many college students, I was struggling financially, and was told by some of the women who worked there that the Lusty Lady was a safe environment. The starting wage was $10 an hour; $25 an hour was the top wage. There was no customer contact and the hours were flexible. Because the Lusty Lady was

1

a peep-show, surrounded with mirrors and neon lights, which operated on quarters and dollar bills, the women danced behind glass. I eventually decided to see what the club was all about and scheduled an audition—a week later I was hired by Josephine, a Black manager (called a show director) and former Lusty dancer herself.

In many ways, the club lived up to its reputation as a feminist operation: Women were escorted to their cars at night by male support staff, customers were not allowed to be disrespectful or abusive toward dancers, and overall there was a camaraderie among the dancers that made it a safe and supportive environment. During our 10-minute breaks, coffee and snacks were provided in the dressing room.

Yet, within the first month, I felt there was a major problem in the feminist equation of the Lusty Lady—out of 70 dancers only 10 were women of color, and of these, only 3 were Black. I noticed this while I was on stage; there was usually only one woman of color and four White women. If a Black dancer was performing, White (and some Asian) customers often would leave the window and move to one where a White woman was standing, sometimes talking with other White dancers, and ignoring the customer all together. In an extreme case, a White man wanted his $5 back after placing it in the bill collector, and the window revealed a dark-skinned, curvy Black woman. The degree of symbolic anti-Black racism at the Lusty Lady often was overwhelming, but not discussed among the White, Black, and non-Black dancers of color.

However, the full impact of the racism at the club was the issue of Black women performing in what was called "Private Pleasures," a booth that was separate from the main stage, but a more lucrative way for dancers to perform, with wages starting at $5 for 3 minutes; dancers could make up to $60 an hour. I told Josephine that I was interested in working in the booth; she trained me, and the following week I was placed on the schedule. However, I was only scheduled on a "Private Pleasures" shift once, whereas other dancers worked there as often as three or four times a week. I noticed that although non-Black women of color worked in this booth, Black dancers were never scheduled. When I asked Josephine about this, she explained that because White men would pay 25 cents to see us on stage, as opposed to the $5 required in the "Private Pleasures" booth, having Black women dance in the booth would lead to the club loosing money.

I couldn't believe what I was hearing: Without any evidence of what these customers preferred, she controlled the degree to which Black women could work within the club. If Black women were having a hard time gaining customers in the "Private Pleasures" booth, how would limiting our exposure help? Shortly after this conversation, I asked the other two Black dancers to join me in a meeting with the show director. This meeting resulted in an agreement that a Black dancer would be rotated in the booth schedule once a week for 3 months to measure customer response. It was a form of affirmative action, but only on a probationary basis. I mentioned the problem of Black women not being allowed to dance in the booth to some of the White dancers. Although they agreed this was an unfair policy, they largely saw it as our issue and wished us well. Although this was one of the most obvious examples of discrimination within the workplace, it was not the issue that sparked the union movement. That issue, instead, involved customers videotaping dancers through the one-way windows behind which they danced. Although the customers could see and videotape the dancers, the dancers could only see their own reflections.

Dancers at the Lusty Lady quickly organized to inform management that they wanted a no-camera policy for customers, as well as removal of the one-way windows so they could see who was watching them. They started to question other issues in the workplace, such as not being able to call in sick (at least without fear of losing their jobs), or having to find dancers who resembled them physically to replace a shift if they could not come to work, which was difficult for women of color to do. In order to deter the dancers from unionizing, management made two concessions: They replaced the one-way windows and they scheduled Black dancers in the booth. Despite these concessions, many of us knew unionization would be our only protection against management abuses.

We sought legal advice from the Exotic Dancers Alliance and were put in contact with our union representative, Stephanie Bailey. The process of unionizing with SEIU Local 790 was exciting, but also hard work, including long nights at the bargaining table, media coverage, strikes and lock outs, deciding what we wanted in our first contract. However, during that time, I remember fighting to have race recognized as a real issue for exotic dancers of color, and not eclipsed by the aforementioned issues that many White dancers viewed as the "larger," more important issues and were largely quoted in the local and national newspapers covering the unionization.

The unionization of the Lusty Lady really put the issue of sex work on the table, not only for the labor movement, but also in feminist and queer communities, both of which have had rocky relationships with sex work (the feminists often question whether sex work is exploitative, and some queer circles question whether lesbians performing sex work for men are "selling out"). Unionization was a big win for the sex workers movement, and yet some unfinished business remains: the role of race and stratification in U.S.-based sex work, especially exotic dancing.

While working as a union organizer I noticed that the San Francisco clubs where many women of color worked were located in seedy areas surrounded by fast food restaurants, check-cashing venues, and drug dealers.

These clubs also had the worst working conditions: coerced prostitution, police raids, stage fees as high as $160 a shift, and sexual harassment from management. The women who worked at these clubs were mostly women of color, with few White women; many were single mothers and immigrants. Even though I am proud of the work my co-workers and I did at the Lusty Lady, I recognize that we were in a very privileged position because, unlike most exotic dancers, we were legally classified as employees, we didn't have physical contact with customers, we didn't pay stage fees, and the club is located in a the North Beach district, a desirable tourist area of San Francisco.

It is a somber fact that after the union, the club hired more Black women in its fourteen-year history, only to have many leave because they did not understand their rights under the contract; some were fired for being late and felt they had no recourse; some left because of dancer racism (i.e., some White dancers objected to rap or hip-hop (the kind that is not sexist) being played because they felt it was violent music). Based on the racism I experienced working as a Black exotic dancer, I wanted to know what happens when one is considered not good enough to be objectified. Many White, middle-class feminists (both those who are pro- and those who are anti-sex work) often assume all women are afforded the same opportunities for employment in the sex industry. This just isn't so.

The following questions will be addressed in this book: What happens to the many Black women and other women of color who are rejected after auditioning to work as strippers in clubs, especially high-end clubs where the dancers are mainly White? How does racial stereotyping affect the many urban Black women and darker-skinned Latina women who work in clubs located in unsafe environments? How do customers respond to the bodies of dark-skinned women? How much money do these women make compared with each other and their White counterparts? How is desire produced by management? What about racial passing? What are the consequences for this type of racial/gender stratification? Does this type of racism affect men of color who work in these clubs? How do racial stereotypes affect women of color in the exotic dance industry? What is management's view on race and the hiring of dancers? What types of capital are being exchanged between dancers and customers? How do racial stereotypes affect women dancing in lesbian clubs?

My aim in this book is to examine the intersections of race, class, and gender as they relate to the types of erotic capital exchanged between Black women and non-Black Latina women within the exotic dance industry. I use a case study analysis of two racially stratified exotic dance clubs in Manhattan and the Bronx, New York, and a lesbian club in Oakland, California. I illustrate how erotic capital functions, on both an institutional and a symbolic level, within the clubs, with attention to the following themes: constructions of whiteness among dancers of color, pay differences among dancers, and safety issues for dancers, as well as how these elements work to produce inequalities among Black and Latina women.

Markets of Desire: Race and Gender Stratification

Many feminist sociologists interested in the intersections between gender and sexual economies, both nationally and internationally (Bernstein, 2007; Kempadoo, 1999; Kempadoo & Doezema, 1998), have focused on commercial sexual industries via questions of labor equality, thus expanding the study of women in labor markets. They have underscored how women working in the sex industry are workers and deserve equal rights. Simultaneously, many feminists argue that women cannot assert agency within sexual economies; their belief is that women are victimized and/or controlled by heterosexual male desire that is not in the best interest of women (Barry, 1995; Dworkin, 1981; MacKinnon, 1983;).

On the other side of the debate regarding pornography and other forms of sex work, contemporary feminists have focused on sexual agency and the empowerment of women within sexual economies as an expansion of women's control of their bodies (Barton, 2006; Bradley-Engen, 2009; Chapkis, 1996; Delacoste & Alexander, 1987; Nagel, 1997). However, within the debate regarding sex work there remains a theoretical void in examining U.S.-based racial and sexual hierarchies present within desire industries (Brooks, 1997; Collins, 1990; Hunter, 2002; Miller-Young, 2007), and how these hierarchies mirror existing forms of racial stratification in U.S. institutions.

Racial segregation within social institutions (such as schools, housing, and job markets) is a prevalent theme within current sociological studies of race relations in the contemporary United States. Many sociologists of race examine the ways that Blacks (and other people of color) are excluded from the dominant culture via legalized laws that both exclude them and define them as Black (Dominquez, 1986). The exclusion of Blacks and Latinos, irrespective of class, within the housing market (see Conley, 1999; Drake & Cayton, 1945; Frazier, 1957; Massey & Denton, 1993; Park, Burgess, & McKenzie, 1925; Pattillo-McCoy, 2000; Sternlieb & Beaton, 1972) affects their educational and job positioning within a highly technological-based economy (Bourgois, 1995; Castells, 1989; Waldinger, 1996, 1999; Williams, 1992; Wilson, 1978).

Similarly, in the field of sociology there has not been an analysis of racism within industries of desire akin to the way racial segregation has been studied in other institutions/industries, such as the housing market. Some exceptions to this have been Paul Cressey's (1932) *The Taxi-Dance Hall: A*

Sociological Study on Commercialized Recreation and City Life, which examined the racial, sexual, and geographic social relations in the Chicago taxi-dance halls in the 1920s, and Kevin J. Mumford's (1997) *Interzones: Black and White Sex Districts in Chicago and New York in the Early Twentieth Century*, which traced the development of commercialized leisure urban spaces of the 1920s and the relationship to racial intermixing and miscegenation.

In the field of sociology, the intersections among race, gender, and sexuality have been documented as they pertain to the social policies that govern many poor and working-class Black and Latino/a families, including single mothers (Collins, 1994, 2004; Roberts, 1997). Although scholars have written about the constructed, perceived social deviancy of the sexuality of poor women of color, and the affects of this in many social policy and reform measures (such as former President Bill Clinton's 1996 welfare reform measure), not much has been written about how these perceptions affect this population within markets, especially those that involve selling sexual services.

This volume expands on the sociological literature on racial stratification by examining race and gender relations in two major cities: Oakland, California and New York City, and exploring strip clubs as a type of desire industry. The correlation I demonstrate is that desire industries reproduce notions of race, and that race, as a category, affects social space resulting in stratification and possible inequality.

A Note About Terminology

In this book I use the term *desire industries* to refer to venues that produce sexual images and erotic fantasies for consumption, and are influenced by movies, television, and magazines regarding the creation of notions of attractiveness. Desire industries can include various forms of media and industries, which operate on ideas of desire and attractiveness such as fashion modeling, acting, and selling retail (Benson, 1987). I use the term *racialized desire* to mean a form of desire influenced by racial ideologies regarding sexuality and degrees of attractiveness as grounds for racial status with the potential for sexual reproduction (symbolically and literally).

I am influenced by Pierre Bourdieu's (1984) work on the role of both symbolic and cultural capital in the construction and enactment of taste, class, and distinction. My use of the term *erotic capital* is similar to Adam Green's (2005) use of it as a form of capital that is related across bodies, and what gives bodies value based on a socially constructed ideal model of beauty/attractiveness held by the dominant culture, that is recognized and accepted by the general public. What is considered desirable erotic capital varies across ethnic groups, countries, and time periods; for example, during the 1960s voluptuous women were desired; whereas in 2009 thin women are more desirable. My definition of erotic capital is based on what is considered desirable by dominant standards of beauty within the United States, which often includes someone who is White, young, and/or has a lean body.

However, I depart from Green's definition because I believe that erotic capital also affects the life chances of people, depending on which end of erotic capital they fall, and can reproduce unequal power relations vis-à-vis not just men, but also between other women. Erotic capital can be converted to economic capital, such as social capital, and also can serve as a credit, especially if economic capital is lacking (see Hunter, 2002). Throughout this book I employ the term *racialized erotic capital* to suggest that erotic capital is affected by variables such as weight, skin color, speech patterns, gender presentation, and hair texture.

Being a Woman in the Field

I used a multimethodological approach for my research: I asked interviewees open-ended questions and used media analysis, historical, ethnographic, and participant-observation methods. I studied three clubs: Temptations in the Bronx, Conquest in Manhattan, and Girlielicious, a Black lesbian club in Oakland.[1] I also analyzed the Internet Web sites of these clubs for racial representation of dancers and potential customers.

I conducted 31 interviews with men and women (dancers, customers, and managers) of various races and classes ranging from ages 22 to 45 years.[2] Many of the dancers I interviewed in New York were students at colleges within the City University of New York (CUNY) system.

As a young Black woman conducting research, I came across some challenges in the field regarding gaining and maintaining access to individual sites. For example, my demeanor (college-educated, status as researcher, conservative dress, young, Black, single woman, and feminine exterior) sometimes proposed problems for me maintaining access to Temptations in the Bronx. When I first started researching the site, managers, bouncers, and the one doorwoman, a Latina who worked at the front desk, welcomed my presence—even when I told them I was a researcher, which often makes people who run strip clubs nervous, especially if illegal activity is going on. However, after a short time there, the manager told me I needed to be accompanied by a man in order to enter the club. I felt this rule was created for me because some people were suspicious of me interviewing there. I did not have any problems as a single woman interacting with customers at Conquest, my presence was welcomed as long as I did not visibly take notes or make customers or dancers feel uncomfortable. I usually spoke to dancers on their break; I spoke to customers at the bar while they were drinking and talking with the bartenders.

At the Oakland research site I met my interviewees by joining them on the dance floor or while sitting at the bar, and after explaining my project. When interviewing women customers at the club, I chose to introduce myself as a lesbian sociologist interested in gender roles among women in Oakland's queer community; when talking to dancers, I changed my description and said I was interested in the benefits of being a dancer for women versus men, and sometimes mentioned that I used to be a dancer to gain their trust. I had a challenging time interviewing dancers because they were performing, and often in a rush, thus the reason I have more interviews with female customers.

Another problem I ran into was one of safety. As a lesbian, I did not always have a male partner to accompany me during field research. I also didn't have a car, so I relied on public transportation; this was not so much of a problem in New York where subways run all night, although when the crowd became rowdy at Temptations I found myself leaving as early as 8 p.m. to take the subway home.

The last challenge I had concerned financing my research. Because I did not receive a grant to conduct my research, I personally paid the entry fees for the expensive clubs like Conquest, where it was $30 (at both Temptations clubs and Conquest was $11), a glass of water at Conquest was $10, and lap dances at both clubs were $20, although I only got lap dances at Conquest as a way to talk to dancers, because at Temptations I could talk to both dancers and customers at the bar.

Outline of This Book

Chapter 1 examines the historical development of burlesque into striptease and the existing stigma around the performance, and the current zoning laws of New York regarding operation of strip clubs enforced by Mayor Rudy Giuliani in 1995. I give a brief overview of the zoning laws, and the impact they have had on the strip club industry. In chapter 2, I explore the geographic areas of industries of desire within a historical urban context, providing historical background to the South Bronx, which is where Temptations is located, and Conquest, which has two locations in Manhattan. I map out the racial and class demographics of the two clubs examining dancer and customer interactions. I also examine the role of customers' taste and consumer choices.

In chapter 3, I illuminate the ways customer interaction allows for some women of color to transcend their social, symbolic, and economic status by accessing levels of cultural capital that would otherwise not be available to them, which helps them educationally and economically.

Chapter 4 examines the intersection of erotic capital and gender relations within same-sex women spaces of erotic performances; I explore differences and similarities between these queer spaces and straight clubs. I also analyze the issue of violence among women in these spaces and how that mirrors overall systemic disinvestment and violence within the communities in which these clubs exist.

In Chapter 5, I use content analysis of club Web sites to argue that the racial advertising on the Internet of women who work at Temptations, Conquest, and Girlielicious is coded in racial and class terms, geared to attract a particular clientele and situate these clubs within a larger spatial relationship to urban space. I focus on the racial choice of women used to advertise both Temptations and Conquest. I also examine differences between the marketing techniques of same-sex clubs, such as Girlielicious versus straight clubs like Temptations and Conquest to explore how various kinds of erotic capital are advertised and how advertising geared toward a female audience differs than that geared primarily toward men. In Chapter 6, I make connections between the geographic environments of Temptations and Conquest while exploring the relationship to larger patterns of racialized segregation and job stratification in the lives of the dancers, customers, and managers of these clubs.

I conclude with a discussion of the consequences for Black and Latina stratification in the exotic dancer industry based on erotic capital and what this could mean regarding social policies relating to welfare, reproductive rights, violence in the lives of Black and Latina working-class women, and post-Civil Rights racial discourse.

1

A History of Desire Industries in New York City

Burlesque, the Public Sphere, and the Construction of Morality

The club was very working class, most dancers had kids; some were on drugs . . . a lot of grinding and touching. There were all kinds of women: light-skinned Italian women, Black skinny busty women. There were actually more White women at that time than women of color. I feel that in 2003 the market started going down; that was the summer I got hired at Conquest—when they started to hire more women of color, and bend a little on their image. The image now is White women with skinny bodies, blonde hair, and big boobs.

—Cristina (24-year-old Puerto Rican dancer at Conquest)

In order to discuss the current status of stripping and exotic dance clubs in New York, it is important to understand the history of stripping in New York, as it evolved from burlesque, and larger theater movements, ranging from associations with high- and lower-class entertainment, gentlemen's clubs of the 1950s, to racial- and class-based associations with poverty, and social deviancy in the 1970s, to the current stratification of exotic dancers based on race and class.

An examination of desire industries in New York City pertaining to dancing dates back to 1868 with the rise of burlesque entertainment performed by English entertainer Lydia Thompson and her female troupe, the British Blondes. During this time, New York City was a thriving place for theatrical entertainment, with burlesque being one of many types.

According to Robert C. Allen (1991) burlesque was

One instance of nineteenth-century American theatrical culture, burlesque must be considered in light of the fundamentally ambiguous and contradictory place that theater—as social institution and abstract concept—occupied in American culture from the colonial period almost to the Civil War. (p. 45)

Burlesque was part of a radical cultural transformation of U.S. theater culture, especially in New York. In New York City, popular theaters during the mid-19th century included the Bowery, Astor Place Theater, Broadway Theater, and the Academy of Music. The advent of burlesque challenged Victorian expectations for urban women in public space regarding appearance and behavior, as well as women's presence on stage.[1] Historically, burlesque originated in the 1840s during the Victorian era and underscored class tensions between the working classes and the rules of respectability dictated by the aristocracy. Theatrical performances (which became popular in the 1820s) of any kind were looked down upon by the aristocracy because of the association between actors on stage and exchanging their talent for money—which also was associated with prostitution.

Allen argues that burlesque transformed from a theatrical form in which women entertainers challenged middle-class norms regarding female sexuality, thus creating a spectacle centered on the sexual display of women. Thus, the display of women on stage created anxiety for Puritans concerned with proper gender roles, whereas the role of men as audience members and onstage was slowly becoming more accepted.[2] Women were allowed to perform on stage as long as they did so in ways that did not challenge dominant gender ideologies (i.e., performing in melodramas and ballets). In the pre-Civil War era melodrama was the dominant mode of theater performance.

The melodrama consisted of a hero and a heroine and revolved around romantic love, thus illustrating notions of acceptable heterosexual gender roles and a contained female sexuality. Women in melodrama usually were displayed as virtuous and spiritual, and their bodies were fully covered by long dresses exuding elements of true Victorian womanhood. The ballet, which originated in Europe, involved dance and the exposure of women's bodies unlike that of melodrama. This exposure created anxiety for bourgeoisie audience members who were still invested in Victorian values regarding the female body on stage and traditional gender roles; many reformers encouraged women to boycott ballets, thus resembling vice reformers of the late 19th century.

One way ballet was made acceptable to moral reformist was within the realm of romanticism—its association with high art, and a highlighting of stage plots, and

portraying evanescent sprites and bewitched shepherdesses—unattainable and in some cases nonhuman ideals of beauty and grace. Ballet became morally and socially acceptable . . . by containing the ballerina within a silent, removed world; within plots that alluded to the settings of high-art literature and painting; and within a body that promoted rather than detracted from the illusion that the audience was watching a creature with the same materiality as a fairy. (Allen, 1991, p. 91)

The next mode of performance during the 1830s involving women being onstage was living pictures, which was viewed as the prelude to burlesque,[3] and consisted of performers imitating paintings and/or statues surrounded by scenery and stage props. Eventually, nudity was included with stage mangers representing statues and paintings of nude (often male) subjects. However, in the 1840s, a shift from male to female subjects occurred, making living pictures more condemned in the eyes of the public—the explosion of human-ized art augmented the numbers of female models. Similar to efforts made from anti-vice squads to remove prostitution from urban streets, city officials attempted to suppress living picture exhibitions, but they were able to survive by blending into the lower-tier working-class venues of entertainment such as storefront windows, museums, and concert saloons.

The final prelude to what Allen refers to, as "Thompsonian burlesque," was the 1861 performance of Jewish actress Adah Menken in the play *Mazeppa*,[4] who according to Allen was "the first American theatrical star not to run away from the charges of moral and social transgressiveness that were almost sure to attach themselves to a popular actress" (p. 97). Menken was known for her independence and for combining feminine sexuality and speech, and succeeding within mainstream theater. In addition to *Mazeppa*, the 1866 musical, *The Black Crook,* which opened on Broadway in New York City and was considered the first musical, also featured women on stage in ballet attire, which by this time was association with high-art, but the play was still viewed as pushing the moral boundaries of respectable images of womanhood because the dancers wore flesh-colored tights.

Theaters, Space, and Morality

The acceptance of theater as a respectable form of entertainment resulted from tensions between the upper-class that had built and controlled theater performances and audience behavior during the post-revolutionary era, and lower-class audiences who rebelled against bourgeois taste (Allen, 1991, p. 66). One method of making the theater acceptable to the bourgeois, and removing the moral stigma, was to open fine art galleries and museum theaters that consisted of paintings and sculptures appearing as an educational institution—all appealing to elite taste. The geographic space of the theater also was organized by class distinctions and consisted of the following three areas: the ground-level pit, the boxes, and the gallery.

The gallery was not only reserved for prostitutes, but in the South was reserved for house slaves, and in the North for free Blacks (Allen, 1991). It is interesting to note that Blacks[5] were associated with White prostitutes, reflecting their lower status compared with White propertied men and elite White women.

An event that intensified the class divisions among theatergoers was the 1849 Astor Place Theater riot, which underscored class tensions especially felt by the predominately working-class audience who attended performances at the Bowery Theater. The riot was provoked by the presence of actors William Charles Macready and Edwin Forrest, who were symbols of class rivalry along national lines. Allen (1991) states that the two actors:

> Represented antithetical approaches to acting and to the theater. Macready stood for the integrity of the dramatic text, the actor as scholar, and the theater as cultural shrine. Forrest was Jacksonian masculinity personified: bombastic, direct, flamboyant. To the Bowery pit, the rivalry had come to symbolize a contest between the democratic and popular native son and the aristocratic Englishman. (p. 59)

The Astor Place riot resulted in greater management control, audience submission, and performances geared less toward a diverse audience; it also meant a more socially conservative environment for burlesque performances. Hence, the emergence of the concert saloon during the 1860s became the venue for shows that appealed to working-class men and included alcohol, female sexuality, and variety shows. Tim Gilfoyle (1992) describes the concert saloons in New York City as "the precursor of modern urban nightlife—the model for vaudeville and the cabaret. Concert saloons were New York's first nightclubs" (p. 224).

Similarly, Allen's (1991) study of concert saloons equated them with immorality and prostitution, stating that the "the focus of bourgeois objections to concert saloons was the waiter girl[6] and her actual possible connection to prostitution" (p. 74). Thus, the location of burlesque performances and afflictions with prostitution added to the moral disapproval of it as a legitimate are form. Andrea Friedman (2000) also contends that burlesque catered to a more sex-oriented audience, whereas vaudeville attracted a family-oriented audience.

Transformation of Burlesque: Race, Gender, and Genre

During the post-Civil War epoch, burlesque represented two subgenres based on use of humor and parody mocking the middle class and displaying the female figure. The humor in burlesque developed in large part from minstrel shows featuring female minstrels, and also involved racial representation of people of color as the "Other." Burlesque and minstrel performances both involved mockery of bourgeoisie values,[7] and an embodiment of what was publicly considered "grotesque." In discussing the class critique of minstrel performances, literary critic, Jules Zanger (1974), argues that in minstrel shows the interlocutor was a caricature of upper-class U.S. society.

This racial representation of blackface in minstrel performances combined with the portrayal of [White] women's bodies in burlesque[8] creates an opportunity for observing racial hierarchies and positioning in burlesque. The representation of racial "Others" is critical in constructing desire; whereas burlesque performers did not perform in blackface, the White female performers did perform caricatures of non-White racial groups, such as Native Americans. During the late 19th century and into the 20th century, the creation of world exposition tours (such as the World's Columbian Exposition of 1893) and the field of anthropology, influenced burlesque, especially concerning the sexual display of women's bodies (Allen, 1991).

The expositions displayed a cornucopia of people from "exotic places" and a place where White U.S. citizens could compare their culture to other villages from around the world. However, the fairs also were seen as a way to represent the non-White world as savage, supported with scientific evidence (i.e., anthropology, eugenics) of racial inferiority (Rydell, 1984). Similarly, Anne McClintock (1995) argues that the world fair expositions and exhibitions represented a globalized form of consumerism, in addition to colonial conquest.

Race and gender spectacles emerged along with national and global consumerism[9]; however, these forms of spectacles are represented differently along race and gender categories. According to Allen (1991), "reliance on sexual display in burlesque greatly increased after the Chicago World's Columbian Exposition of 1893. It was here that the 'cooch' dance [belly dancing] was introduced to American audiences" (p. 225). The cooch dance was the prelude to the striptease, and was part of the exposition, which contributed to a colonial hierarchy of race. Gail Bederman (1995) argues:

> The exposition was based on turn-of-the-century assumptions about White supremacy and manhood; indeed, the grounds were divided into two racially specific areas: the White City and the

Midway Plaisance. Whereas the White City depicted the mil-
lennial advancement of white civilization, the Midway Plaisance
presented the undeveloped barbarism of uncivilized dark races.
(p. 31)

Therefore, the cooch dance was associated with the Midway (Jarrett, 1997). Thus, the association with freak shows, race, and lower-class
status became apparent with the display of female "primitive" exotic others.
Allen (1991) discusses the phenomena of the freak show consisting of
human curiosities, such as cooch dancers, Siamese twins, hermaphrodites,
and people with skin disorders, the most famous being the Elephant Man
(John Merrick). Racialized advertisements of burlesque illuminate the fact
that bodies of color experience a different type of objectification than White
women—which is true of contemporary exotic dancing and other types of
sex work. One example of this is in posters advertising burlesque shows; one
poster entitled, "The Beautiful Indian Maidens," where "a tribe of Amazonian
Indian warriors gather at a riverbank. In the background a stag flees for his
life from his spear-hurling female pursuers, while in the foreground one of
the huntresses hold her catch by neck, displaying it for the viewer: a tiny,
duck-headed, tuxedo-clad man" (Allen, 1991, p. 206).
    Similar to the way minstrel performances provided an avenue for Whites
to reinforce White supremacy and to project hidden desires, ideologies, and
fantasies via the performance of blackface (Roediger, 1999), this burlesque
advertisement uses race to reinforce the transgressive nature of the White
burlesque dancers via an exotic other, in this case Native Americans, who
were seen as savage and barbaric vis-à-vis the civilized White ruling elite.
Hence, this creates a stratification based on race (and class) of ways women
in desire industries are positioned differently based on these variables—a
point that is explored in more detail later in this book.
    In 1893, the cooch dance moved to New York after the exposition closed,
and was more sexualized since becoming a part of burlesque performance; it
was largely associated with working-class male audiences until 1916 when it
spread to upscale Broadway cabarets (Erenberg, 1981; Friedman, 2000). During
the 20th century, burlesque continued as a form of entertainment and with
industrialization in the 1900s, consumer patterns became more upscale and tied
to taste and consumer identity[10] (Bernstein, 2007; Frank, 2002). According to
Katherine Frank, these developments "positioned women as both consumers
themselves and as objects to be consumed, and as women increasingly entered
the workplace and leisure sphere in this context, entertainment styles were
transformed" (p. 43). However, Kevin Mumford (1997) argues that this process
was racialized with White women gaining the most access to the public sphere,
especially as prostitution became associated with Black women.

During this time, the Ziegfeld Follies[11] represented an acceptable form of feminine sexual display and "blended into the ideology of bourgeois consumer culture" (Allen, 1991, p. 245). In the mid-1910s, stock burlesque formed as a result of movie theaters and cabarets, where the performance of burlesque was stripped down to its bare essentials, incorporating striptease. According to Lucinda Jarrett (1997), in the 1920s class "increasingly became an issue in theatre licensing" as upscale cabarets were granted liquor licenses, whereas venues that housed burlesque were not (p. 107). Friedman states that striptease developed from burlesque during the 1930s and involved new ways of performing that included the stripper taking off most of her clothes while on stage. She would have her breast covered and wore a G-string and/or panties or a leotard.

In the 1930s, while surviving the economic downfall of the Great Depression,[12] burlesque received opposition from anti-vice groups in New York. As a result of social crackdowns from middle-class anti-vice groups, burlesque eventually disappeared and strip clubs came on the scene (Allen, 1991; Friedman, 2000; Jarrett, 1997).

Burlesque theaters were seen by the 42nd Street Property Owners' Association as lower property values because they attracted undesirable customers to the Times Square area, despite the fact that customers of various class backgrounds attended burlesque performances (Friedman, 2000). Burlesque theaters were in jeopardy of losing their licenses if the performances were believed to be obscene. Thus, in order for burlesque to continue and to be approved by city officials, the sexual style and humor associated with it and with striptease was banned, especially during World War II, when it was viewed as undermining the virility of the men who had the responsibility of defending the country (Friedman, 2000).

Gentleman's Clubs, Strip Clubs, and Zoning Laws in New York

In the 1950s, during the consumer boom of World War II, strip clubs came to represent, as they did in the early 20th century, a symbol of upscale consumer status. The 1950s introduction of *Playboy Magazine*, and its advertising to a middle-class male, influenced the presence of gentleman's clubs, or Playboy clubs, in the 1960s, starting in Chicago (Frank, 2002). According to Frank, Playboy clubs featured "scantily clothed women and offered somewhat respectable, upscale, masculinized entertainment that had links to other forms of consumption—plush atmosphere, steaks, liquor, pornography—and indeed, to a mythologized lifestyle" (p. 50). Playboy clubs eventually were pushed out of the market; however, aspects of these clubs were recreated in what is now called "gentleman's clubs," referring to upscale strip clubs.

The racialization of the term *exotic dancer* was prevalent during this time (probably because stereotypes of people of color were still very popular in the media); hence, dancers used "jungle themes" during their performances, which mirrored the eroticization of people of color during the world exposition (Jarrett, 1997).

During the 1970s, more women began working at strip clubs because of the recession and thus, these clubs increasingly became associated with moral vices, such as drug use, prostitution, and crime[13] (Delany, 1999; Frank, 2002). In the 1980s, as more women worked in the exotic dance industry, and the service-sector expanded, club management, starting with San Francisco's Mitchell Brother's Theater, began charging dancers a stage fee that ranged anywhere from $40 to $250 depending on the club. Dancers were expected to pay the fee out of their tips at the end of their shift. The instituting of stage fees led to the economic pressures for dancers to prostitute in order to make the stage fee, thus adding to this image of deviancy and crime.

According to anthropologist Judith Hanna (1998):

> because of their working-class associations and the persistent, perhaps erroneous belief that they are indelibly linked to prostitution, crime, and negative secondary effects, establishments that feature forms of striptease have already been subject to more severe regulations (especially regarding alcohol and nudity) than other kinds of entertainment and some municipalities have attempted to use restrictive regulation to close down the businesses altogether. (p. 62)

This association with deviancy is underscored in continued zoning regulations and the closing of strip clubs in urban areas, such as New York City. Samuel Delany (1999) examines this connection with strip clubs, porn shops, and vice in New York City's Times Square area during the beginning of the AIDS crisis stating, "The threat from AIDS produced a 1985 health ordinance that began the shutdown of the specifically gay sexual outlets in the neighborhood: the gay movie houses and the straight porn theaters" (p. 5).

In 1995, as part of a plan to make Times Square "family-friendly" for middle-class White property owners, Giuliani enforced zoning laws forbidding strip clubs from being within 500 feet of schools, churches, day-care centers, or residential buildings.

The criminalization of desire industries, along with intersections of racism, classism, and geographic location, adds to isolation of people and the disruption of communities. In *The Life and Death of Great American Cities*, Jane Jacobs (1965) describes what happens to communities when buildings are torn down and people displaced. According to Jacobs, lack of street-level business and diversity produces lack of human traffic, and self-policing, so that strangers are mixed in with long-term residents, and social networks begin to break down. Delany further reinforces this point by stating, "such turnovers produce the dangerous neighborhoods: the housing project, the park with not enough stores and eating spaces bordering on it, the blocks and blocks of apartment residences without any ameliorating human services" (p. 154).

This last point is critical to understanding how zoning laws, along with systemic disinvestment in low-income communities of color, affects workers in desire industries, and the larger community that surrounds them. It also affects how customers view strip clubs and the value placed on the women who work in them regarding safety and wages.

2

Marketing Desire and Geographic Coding in the Bronx

We are in the South Bronx; you know what I'm saying. We ain't got the money to do all that much advertising. It's often word of month. People come in and tell their friends . . . we get a lot of customers and workers that way.

—Tommy (Caribbean manager at Temptations)

Temptations is located in the South Bronx even though the address was on Park Avenue—might lead potential customers to think it is in Manhattan. Once when I called the club asking for directions and whether the club was in the Bronx, I was told by a woman whom I assumed was Latina by her accent, that it was on Park Avenue. When I wanted more specific directions, she said, "What more do you want to know? Park Avenue." She would not say that the club was actually in the Bronx. However, on another occasion, a different woman answered when I called and told me the address. She added that the club is located in the Bronx. This dilemma of whether or not Temptations is located in the South Bronx has to do with what the reputation of the South Bronx is versus that of Park Avenue.

Park Avenue begins at 8th Street at Fourth Avenue, turns into Park Avenue South at 17th Street, and becomes Park Avenue proper at 33rd Street. It ends at 132nd Street, however, it continues into the Bronx, where Temptations is located. Park Avenue is known for high real estate prices and being the location of large corporations, such as JP Morgan Chase and Citigroup. A one-bedroom apartment on Park Avenue rents for $2,400 a month. According to the 2004 U.S. Census Bureau, Manhattan had an overall median income of $47,030 and a population of 1,562,723. The Upper East Side alone had an income of $90,000 per capita and a population of 100,000 compared with the Bronx, which had a median income of $27,611 and a population of 1,365,536. The South Bronx itself had a population of 135,699 and a median income of $20,809. Given this information, one can conclude that club promoters at Temptations would try to gain a sense of prestige from being on Park Avenue, despite not being located on Park Avenue proper.[1]

History of the South Bronx

Originally, Native American tribes (the Mohegans, Weckquaesgeeks, Siwanoy, Sint Sincs, Kitchenwonks, Manhattan, Tankitekes, and Taekmucks) inhabited the South Bronx until the Dutch settled it in 1639 (Jonnes, 2002). During the mid-1800s Irish, German, Italian, and Jewish immigrants came to New York in search of a better life, escaping from poverty, political, and religious persecution. The Irish and Germans soon moved into the Bronx; Irish men were doing manual labor (some opened businesses) and the Germans farmed and opened their own breweries and churches (Jonnes, 2002; Waldinger, 1996). As the New York economy expanded with industry, questions regarding immigration and assimilation became more prevalent as immigrants from Europe came to Ellis Island and lived in the Lower East Side before moving to the Bronx (Park, 1925). There also was concern regarding the crime that resulted from the poor living conditions of the immigrants (Jonnes, 2002; Sugrue, 1993).

During the early 1900s, the Bronx became more urbanized; Yankee Stadium was built in 1923, and the Grand Concourse, which supposedly resembled Paris' Champs-Élysées and the Concourse Plaza, was constructed in 1924 (Jonnes, 2002). Italian and Jewish immigrants also moved from the Lower East Side to the Bronx.[2] Like the rest of New York, the Bronx was greatly affected by the Great Depression of the 1930s and depended on President Franklin Roosevelt's New Deal programs for survival. The Triborough Bridge was built in 1936, connecting Manhattan and Queens; and the streets of the South Bronx were no longer quiet (Jonnes, 2002).

A second wave of immigration hit New York during World War II. Rather than Europeans, these immigrants and migrants were Blacks from the South and Puerto Ricans. The Black migrants settled in Harlem[3] and the Puerto Ricans in Spanish Harlem, Mott Haven, Hunts Point, and later Charlotte Street in the Bronx, thus joining the Irish and Jewish residents (Jonnes, 2002). According to Jonnes:

> The postwar influx of demobilized vets, blacks and Puerto Ricans forced New York City to wrestle once more with its perennial housing problems . . . as the offspring of the European immigrants decamped, the Puerto Ricans and blacks snapped up their vacated

apartments. Overcrowding, and the newcomers' sheer poverty, transformed decent neighborhoods into slums . . . the solution seemed obvious to City officials—housing projects. (p. 102)

When Puerto Ricans began moving in, White gangs formed in opposition to their presence; simultaneously landlords preferred renting to Puerto Ricans because they were considered more desirable than U.S. Blacks (Jonnes, 2002). By the 1960s, poverty was setting in along with the construction of housing projects, a flourishing drug trade (largely heroin), and White flight.[4]

The location of Temptations mirrors what Roderick Wallace (1990) refers to as desertication: the process of depopulation and destabilization of neighborhoods as abandonment, economic disinvestment, and decline occurs.[5] Doug Massey and Nancy Denton (1993) discuss the impact of this type of residential disinvestment, especially concerning Black segregation:

> No group in the history of the United States has ever experienced the sustained high level of residential segregation that has been imposed on blacks in large American cities for the past fifty years. This extreme racial isolation did not just happen; it was manufactured by Whites through a series of self-conscious actions and purposeful institutional arrangements that continue today. (p. 2)

This economic concentration of racialized poverty existed throughout the 1980s and 1990s, and continues in to the present day, despite grassroots organizations to counter it. This is the history of the area that surrounds Temptations, the adjacent neighborhoods, such as Mott Haven and Hunts Point, and the context for the dancers, managers, and customers who work at and patronize the club.

A Journey Down to the South Bronx

I am curious to see what a gentleman's club in the Bronx can say about the history of people in the neighborhood, about gender occupation, consumption, race, and urban space. I pass a local McDonald's where teenagers are hanging out; people getting off work and mothers pushing baby strollers are picking up a fast-food dinner.

The street is busy and people dash in and out of the Chase Manhattan Bank while taxis honk to see if someone needs a ride to a destination.

There is a Black homeless woman standing outside of the bank, as I cross the street toward her, I hand her $1, and she responds with a smile and a compliment on my dreadlocks. I walk pass an H&R Block, Burger King, T & L nail salon, law offices, the Montefiore Medical center, Dunkin' Donuts, the Bronx Museum of Arts, and the Yankee Tavern, and head toward the Court House, where people are still leaving work. The people in the area are mostly Black and Latino/a and working class. After walking five blocks, I see just one White male dressed in a suit leaving the Court House. I keep walking past Grand Concourse Plaza, which is a mall consisting of a movie theater, numerous clothing stores, including Ashley Stewart, a store for plus-size women, Payless shoe store, and a Pet Land pet store.

I stop in a pharmacy to ask for directions because it doesn't seem as if Park Avenue is any where near where I am. I am told by a Latina that it is a couple of blocks down; I am currently on East 161st Street. I ask her if she knows the area well, and what the racial make-up is. She smiles saying that she doesn't know because she lives in a different area of the Bronx, however, the pharmacist, an Asian man, tells me it's a mixed area with many different types of Blacks, Latinos, and Whites. "The only group that is not here really is Asian," he replies packaging a bottle of pills. I thank him and decide to get into one of the many town cars, which are the neighborhood cabs, honking for potential passengers.

I hail a cab driven by a young Latino guy and tell him the area I am going to, and he tells me I am actually quite a ways from it as we pass an Associate Supermarket and Melrose Job Center. I ask him if he has been in the area long; like many people here he has. I feel comfortable with him and tell him I am going to Temptations, and he tells me he picks up many customers coming or going from the club. "What is this club like?" I asked, eager to know what I should expect in terms of the crowd.

"It's nice. More upscale than the other clubs here in the Bronx, especially in Hunts Point. It's safe. The only fights actually are between the other dancers, rather than with the men who go in."

"What are some of the other clubs in the area?" I asked

"There's the G-Spot, Sexy Dancers, Player's Club, the Triangle, the Gentlemen's Club, and the Golden Ladies."

"Which clubs would you say are classier?"

"I would say that the club you are going to is . . . a gentlemen's club, and the Player's Club is good . . . but the others are more low class. Some are bars that serve alcohol, like the Triangle, so they attract a different, rowdier crowd."

This hierarchical ranking of clubs, according to the cab driver, resembles the overall ranking of the South Bronx compared with other parts of the Bronx, which is characterized by White flight, economic disinvestment in

the area, drugs, and high crime rates. In terms of sex work, street prostitution sometimes occurs in exchange for drugs or money for basic survival;
men can buy oral sex services for as low as $5.[6] This club ranking also
makes a statement about race and poverty because strip clubs reflect aspects
of social class, which is tied to notions of race regarding who works there
and who goes there, thus reflecting the level of classiness and desirability
of a club.[7]

As we are driving past Willis Avenue, I notice that the area is a little
more deserted than near the old Yankee Stadium, where I was initially. We
finally arrive and I see an old skating building and Latina women smoking
outside of the clubs, as well as a few men, whom I assume, based on their
size and the way they are dressed, are the bouncers. I pay the driver $7 and
get out. He gives me his card and tells me to call him anytime I am in the
area because this is where he is on duty.

I thank the cab driver and walk toward the people standing outside
the club.

While walking around the area I take note of the surrounding institutions
and businesses: Hostos Community College, a Medicare health rehabilitation
service center, a sign advertising for taxi drivers, the Triborough Bridge, a
diner, a public auto auction, a car wash/muffler repair shop, and a Kentucky
Fried Chicken. There are no banks anywhere in sight, but there are many
check-cashing places. South of Temptations is the Mott Haven neighborhood,
which contains housing projects and more local business, although many
buildings and businesses had been abandoned and are boarded up. I was very
aware of my gender, and to a lesser degree my race, while walking around
the area as men in cars honked their horns: some cabs, others just regular
cars. Compared with Manhattan and Brooklyn, this is the most experience
I have had with men honking their horns, which suggests that this area of
the Bronx has more of a car culture than other parts of New York, with the
exception of residential areas in Queens near the airports.

Race, Gender, and Erotic Capital at Temptations

Once inside Temptations, a Black bouncer named Rob, who told me there
is no cover before 7 p.m.; after 7, it's $20, greeted me. He assumed I was
looking for work and asked me if I wanted to fill out a job application; I told
him no, and explained that I was there to check out the club. He responded
by laughing and telling me, "Fine, go right ahead, we don't discriminate
against anyone here, we get lesbians sometimes." I found it interesting that
he assumed I was a lesbian, because many strip clubs that cater to men will
not allow women in when they are not accompanied by men.[8] Temptations

has two stages, a circular bar that seats 10 customers, a big-screen television showing baseball, and an ATM to the right of it.

For dancers, erotic capital is marketed in four ways:

1. the DJ advertising their dance set,

2. stage lighting,

3. striptease, and

4. soliciting lap dances before or after their performance.

The role of the DJ is to play songs that will complement the dancer's body and movement on stage. The dancer usually selects three 5-minute songs to be played during her set. Most dancers have not had professional dance lessons, although some have had some formalized training.

The stage lighting consists of dim, sultry lights ranging in greens, purples, and reds, which make the dancers appear sexy and create a sensual mood between the audience and the dancer. Dancers market their erotic capital by performing a striptease, usually down to a thong, and walking around before or after their set to see if customers want to buy lap dances. The stage provides the dancer with the most exposure to clientele; the DJ helps by playing music and promoting the dancer before and during her set; the lighting covers up any blemishes that might more visible in bright lights (Frank, 2002).

Some of the dancers wear a variety of outfits designed to tease the customer and to highlight flattering aspects of their bodies. For example, one White woman with a dark tan wore a neon pink gown to highlight her tan under the lights. Other dancers wore form-fitting outfits, and most stripped in a way that teased the customer, then removed their tops, and ending their set by stripping to their underwear or thong.

One Latina dancer dressed as a bride, which I found interesting considering the low societal positioning of working-class exotic dancers, especially those of color, and the contrast to the respectable institution of marriage. I conclude that it is probably the desire to have respect that motivates some of the dancers' choices of outfits that will present them as "respectable" and "classy." I think this is especially true in dancing environments where customers consistently disrespect dancers, something I observed during my visits to Temptations.

There also was a light-skinned Latina dancing to hip-hop on the stage. I watched the men at the bar, many of whom were White, but some were Black and Latino—all appeared to be working-class individuals dressed in jeans and shirts and drinking beer at the bar. Smoking is not permitted and dancers and customers often took smoking breaks outside of the club. I decided to take a seat in front of the bar to take some notes, when I noticed a young Black woman filling out an application.

"Are you filling out an application to dance here?" I ask.

"No, to be a waitress. I was in the restaurant business as a waitress, but now many restaurants aren't hiring, so I want to see if I can be one here."

I smiled at her and wished her luck as I continued taking notes. I look at the other waitresses (all Black and/or Latina) and wondered how they got their jobs at the club. The restaurant is located toward the back of the club, and is not visible from the bar.

I was the only woman customer in the club and a few White guys turned and looked my way; they asked me what I was doing there and I told them I was doing research. "Can I be in your research?" one of them jokingly asked. I smile and entertained their comments before ordering a soda at the bar. The Latina bartender said, "Sorry, honey, I will have to charge you for this . . . it's $7." I told her I understood and gave her the money, as well as a tip. In this environment, my gender sometimes connoted that I should be exempt from paying for drinks depending on the friendliness of the bartender.

I saw the bouncer behind me and decided to ask him a few questions about the club and his experiences there. "I have been here a year. It's okay. I was a security guard at a company in the Bronx before coming here. I am from the Bronx, so it's near where I live," he explained.

When I asked him how long the club had been open, he suddenly became awkward and reserved and said: "See, you're getting personal on me now. You think I didn't notice how you switched up the questions, but I did—now you getting into business. See, I caught that sweetheart. I'm smart."

He then walked away telling me to have a nice day, and that the conservation was over. I found his response strange because the duration of the club's existence is public information that can easily be looked up. However, his response underscored the underground aspect of the sex industry, especially with Giuliani's 1995 zoning laws. Questions about club operations can signify city control or fear of the club being raided by the police and shut down. This is of particular concern for clubs, such as Temptations, that are located in low-income communities of color, where members of the community feel criminalized by the police.

During my visit, I saw a Black man at the bar and assumed he was a customer; he walked over to me and introduced himself as Tommy, one of the co-owners. He is 45 years old and is originally from Trinidad. I introduced myself and explained that I was working on a project regarding men and taste. He smiled at me and told me I could ask him anything I wanted. I was relieved because I somehow managed to alienate the bouncer. I asked him how long the club had been there. "It's 3 years old. I am the co-owner. There are two other guys who own it," he replied. I glanced at the women on stage, most of who were curvy and in good shape; some were thin.

Temptations' owners and promoters tried to distinguish themselves from other clubs in New York, as well as from other clubs in the South Bronx that are known to be seedy and less "classy" and that hire women who, according to Tommy, are not very attractive:

> We hire beautiful women here of all types: Black, Latina, White.
> We wouldn't hire someone who is 300 pounds; she has to be sexy,
> you know? Curvy, not obese. Someone customers wanna see.

Management also distinguished between the kinds of customers they allow into Temptations by enforcing dress codes to keep out those perceived as lower class. While talking in the office he shares with a White manager named John, Tommy explained that they don't allow lower-class customers into the club:

> We have a dress code: no saggy paints or hats turned to the side.
> We don't want the hip-hop crowd, but the classier kind of customer
> who will know how to behave because this is a gentleman's club.
> Men have to be 23 years old to come in and women 21.

A curvy Latina woman with long dark hair came into the office to give John her tip-out[9] and joked with him about what a mean manager he was; to which he replied, "You know you love me." After she left, John said, "She is a lesbian . . . men don't have a chance with her."[10] Tommy continues, "Sometimes the women who come in act as bad as the men. Some are rowdy and loud."

> "Why do you think that is?" I asked.
> "I don't know, but we have to sometimes tell them to
> behave, also."

The idea of women behaving "as bad as men" in the context of acting rowdy or being loud in a place known to be a "male space," illustrates the notion of an "inverted patriarchy," where women try to gain power in male-dominated spaces by taking on the traditional male ways of social interaction.[11] However, during my field research at Temptations, I never observed any rowdy behavior from the female customers toward the dancers.

I thanked Tommy for his time and took a seat at the bar. Tommy's response that the dancers should be "curvy, not obese" illustrates the erotic capital necessary for women to be hired at the club. I sat at the bar and looked around at the customers. There were more White men than I had expected—of 12 men, 8 were White. Of the four men of color, one was Latino and in a wheelchair, and the others were Black. Three White men were sitting near me and one asked what I was doing at the club. We made small talk and I decided to take this as an opportunity to examine why they chose Temptations as opposed to another club, such as Conquest. I discovered by overhearing their conversation that two of the men are brothers; one was a friend . . . all are of Italian heritage from Staten Island. One guy, Bill, a 38-year-old with a girlfriend, told me that he works in the Bronx and sometimes comes to Temptations after work: "I like to stop in every once in a while for a beer and look at the women. I work in the Bronx, so it is convenient."

His 36-year-old unattached brother Daniel, who makes a living by designing Web sites and advertising cell phones as part of his family's business, gave a more nuanced explanation:

> I went to Conquest about 2 years ago, and I didn't like it. I mean first of all it's $60 just to get in. Once you get in, all the women are very money hungry; you could tell they just want your money. I also don't like women with boob jobs, and you could tell a lot of the women had boob jobs, blondes . . . I don't like that. I like women who look more real, like here at Temptations. Also, the other customers . . . they were throwing down $50 bills, $20 bills. They were mostly businessmen. Conquest is not a place for a workingman like me, so I felt uncomfortable by the whole environment. I am shy when it comes to women anyway. I am not outgoing when approaching them.

Mike, a 28-year-old Black male from the Bronx, also found Temptations more comfortable than Conquest, and thought the women had personality despite not being viewed as attractive by mainstream standards:

> I've been to Conquest, and [al]though the women are attractive, it is largely for Caucasian women to work. I like Temptations because the girls got personality, and I don't feel hustled for money there. They go up to me and say "Hey, Mike. How's it going?" I like that. I feel like a person. They wouldn't get hired at a place like Conquest because the club would tell them they would have to lose weight, but I think they are attractive in their own way.

In contrast, Wayne, a 30-year-old Black man I met at Conquest who lives in Harlem had this to say about Temptations:

The women there . . . you could tell they are desperate for money, and sometimes they do things like let you touch them, when they are not supposed to. Also, I didn't like the crowd; the men can be a bit on the rowdy side.

Daniel's response was noteworthy because although he was White, he felt more comfortable at Temptations, which is mostly Black and Latino/a, as opposed to Conquest, which is predominately White, but very middle to upper class regarding dancer appearance and clientele. In this case, class trumped race in terms of comfort level; although he may have had the money to spend at Conquest, he lacked the cultural capital to compete with the businessmen whom he felt had more money to spend.

Wayne's comments regarding taste are similar to Daniel's response. Both Wayne and Daniel felt uncomfortable in the clubs that had dancers who resembled their racial backgrounds. Daniel felt lower class in Conquest and Wayne felt Temptations was too rowdy for his taste. However, there are structural differences between Wayne and Daniel; although both experience racial inconsistency regarding which strip club they felt comfortable attending, Daniel lives in a predominately White area in Staten Island, whereas Wayne lives in Harlem, a predominately Black area—therefore, despite class differences, neighborhood residence influences their experiences as customers.

Daniel encountered a cultural hierarchy during his trip to Conquest, and thus felt like an undesired customer. This cultural hierarchy also reflects the marginalization of dancers and their low erotic capital based on the geographic location and overall positioning of the Bronx in social, racial, and economical terms versus gentlemen's clubs that are located in Manhattan, and that attract men from higher social and economic backgrounds.

Race and Geographic Desire at Conquest

George Chauncey's (1995) *Gay New York: Gender, Urban Culture, and the Making of the Gay Male World, 1890–1940*, documents gay male space in New York City's Greenwich Village; however, recently, there have been clashes between White middle-class heterosexuals moving into the Village and White gay/lesbians in the village regarding the use of the piers by poor young queer people of color. This racial and class tension is highlighted by the establishment of Conquest's location in the Village near surrounding housing projects where poor/working-class Black and Latina/o families live.

According to the 2005 U.S. Census Bureau, the medium family income is $43,434. The racial make up of Manhattan is 98.4% White, 25.3% Black, 0.4% Native, 11.6% Asian, and 27.9% Latino/a.

Conquest gentlemen's club in New York is one of the most famous strip clubs in the country among middle and upper class White men. The original Conquest is located on East 60th Street and charges a $60 cover fee. Within the past 3 years a new location opened on East 28th and charges a $30 cover fee. I decide to attend this new location to conduct research on taste, race, and desire. Conquest is known for its restaurant business in addition to its bar and stage shows. It is also one of the few strip clubs in New York to have survived Giuliani's 1995 zoning laws.

Similar to Temptations, the 28th Street location is near the Expressway Lincoln Tunnel. The Chelsea Piers are a couple of blocks from Conquest; there are bars, restaurants, housing projects, and taxi repair shops. The clubs and bars surrounding Conquest appear to be heterosexual; this is interesting considering that Conquest is located in the Village, which is known for queer clubs and businesses. Adjacent to Conquest is the dance club the Crazy Monkey, which appears to be geared toward heterosexual and predominately White males.

There were only three men standing outside of Conquest when I visited there. I smiled at them and walked through the black doors and a red curtain into the club; a White bouncer greeted me at the door, and a White woman took money from behind a desk. The bouncer stopped me mid-way to ask me if I know what kind of club Conquest is. I told him that I did and explained that I am doing research on men and taste. He seemed relieved and told me he just wanted to make sure I knew that Conquest was a strip club. I assume that with the zoning laws, even a well-respected club such as Conquest can't take any chances. When I paid the woman the $30 cover charge the bouncer asked to see my identification. This experience was different than Temptations where there was no cover in the afternoon, and where I didn't have to show identification the first time I went. I suspect the difference is because managers at Temptations are trying to attract business and because it is located in a low-income Black and Latino/a community, asking for identification and charging high cover fees would deter potential customers who cannot afford to pay a cover, drink fees, and tips for lap dances. Asking for identification could make some customers feel uncomfortable because they may not have the documentation they are being asked for.[12]

When I entered Conquest, I was escorted to a seat at the front of the stage, unlike at Temptations, where I could sit anywhere I wanted, including the bar. At Conquest only dancers occupied the bar, while the customers sat at tables. The seats are a soft reddish color and the tables are round and big enough to hold a couple of glasses. A White waitress came over and asked me if I wanted anything to drink. I ordered a glass of water. She put down a napkin and told me that this time she would give me a glass, however, usually customers order a bottle of water, which is $10. I thanked her and said that next time I would buy a bottle. In Conquest my gender did not evoke economic sympathy or the sense that because I am a woman I might be exempt from paying full price, whereas at Temptations the bartender seemed to regret that she had to charge me for the soda I ordered.

There were 12 dancers working when I was there; most of whom were sitting at the bar, while one was on stage. The dancers were mostly Asian, Latina, and White—I saw only one Black woman who was brown-skinned; there were no dark-skinned women. Most of the dancers also were thin. I noticed a young Asian woman on stage dancing to hip-hop music. Two middle-aged men also are sitting near the stage watching her; one was White and the other was Asian. The dancer moved her hips back and forth to the music. She was wearing a garter with $20 bills attached to her ankle.

The White guy looked bored while he smoked his cigar and constantly checked his watch; the Asian customer seemed to be very interested in the dancer. After her stage show, the dancer got off the stage and gave the Asian customer a lap dance: She was topless and wore only a red thong. The other customer was still acting bored. The customers were mostly White men in their mid-30s to early 50s—the young men dressed more causally in a shirt and jeans, whereas the older men were in suits.

I counted 10 customers and three tables where a woman was present. The customers were White, except for one Black man in his 30s, who was sitting at a table with a White male friend, and the Asian customer. One dancer gave a lap dance to a female customer. At first I thought the female customer was alone, but a man joined her at the table . . . he had apparently stepped out to use the restroom. Both appeared to be enjoying themselves. However, I noticed that I am the only woman who is alone, which made me think of women being in public spaces without the presence of a male. Strip clubs that cater to heterosexual men are traditionally viewed as "male" spaces, where the women who are there are workers, not consumers.

However, in this case it didn't appear as if the female customers needed protection; more like they were companions for the male customers. Having customers bring their female friends/significant others challenges the notion that these men are sneaking out to the strip club without their female partners knowing. This dynamic also can reinforce the virgin–whore dichotomy between the dancer, friend and/or female significant other because the dancer occupies a different category than the other woman regarding status and class. The dancers at Conquest reflect the same, if not higher, class as the women in the audience because they are the club's main attraction, and the women in the audience are there as companions to the male customers. This dynamic also merges the demarcations between public and private spheres regarding heterosexual sexual relationships, where the male customer has "private" sexual relations with his wife/girlfriend, and makes "public" trips to strip clubs usually without the knowledge of his wife/girlfriend (Frank, 2002).

Smoking is allowed in Conquest and cigars are sold in packets behind a glass case at the entrance of the club. While jotting down some notes in my journal, a bouncer came up from behind me and asked what I was doing. I explained that I was doing a study on men and their tastes and apologized for any disturbance I may be causing and that I wouldn't do it if the club were busier. He smiled and told me it was fine; he just wanted to know what I was doing. I am made aware of the precarious position of many strip club owners in light of the zoning laws and that they must be cautious of any activity that may signal undercover cops, or other threats to the business.

However, this experience was different from the one I had with the bouncer at Temptations who stopped talking to me when I asked him questions about the club. At Conquest, the bouncer was only interested in finding out what I was doing; he didn't appear nervous, although taking notes is different than asking direct questions pertaining to club operations.

Advertising Techniques: Race, Space, Class, and Food

One often unrecognized area of marketing for clubs is their menu options; Temptations has a cornucopia of menu selections from which to choose. They offer appetizers such as chicken tenders, buffalo wings, mozzarella cheese sticks, shrimp with tartar sauce, fried shrimp, chicken quesadilla, and a sampler consisting of an assortment of all of them. Soups and salads range from grilled chicken Caesar salad, grilled shrimp salad, Greek salad, soup of the day, and a soup and sandwich combo (sandwiches are burgers, chicken, turkey clubs and grilled cheese sandwiches). Steaks range from top sirloin, rib eye, T-bone, and filet mignon. They also feature chicken and pasta options: lemon caper chicken, boneless chicken breast, grilled chicken, pasta salad, and chicken fettuccine. Seafood consists of the fish of the day, grilled shrimp, and fish and chips. They put an emphasis on the food being served with "the finest of wines and champagnes." Drink names also underscore a Bronx identity, such as "Da Bronx Ice-T."

The menu at Temptations serves the purpose of underscoring feelings of abundance and identity, making the mostly male customers feel they not only can consume women, but food as well. So, food at both clubs helps to underscore the male customer's sense of masculinity and class.[13] Having "fine wines and champagnes" distinguishes Temptations from lower-class clubs, but also suggests the need for status approval by stating such items. The menu also reflects the type of food that may be served in some of the better restaurants in the Bronx. In this context, a regular working-class man is considered "classy" compared with the younger hip-hop crowd that lives in the South Bronx.

Because some of the customers at Temptations are White lower middle-class to working-class men, race also is a factor in their ability to feel comfortable and desirable as a customer. Often, White men (or women) are regarded as more desirable in sex venues occupied by people of color because it is assumed they have money. This observation is very common when examining the racial and class dynamics of international sex and tourist industries in Caribbean islands, such as Jamaica, Cuba, and the Dominican Republic (Bernstein & Schaffner, 2004; Cabeza, 2004; Kempadoo & Doezema, 1998; Puar, 2001).

Although Temptations is not located in a Third World country, it is located in a poor working-class Black and Latino community, and is less expensive than a club like Conquest. It also is located in an area without many restaurants or food options except corner stores that sell liquor, local taquerias, and supermarkets that don't sell organic or gourmet food. Because money is a factor at Conquest regarding how men will be treated as customers by dancers (i.e., if they don't have a lot of money some dancers may quickly leave them for a customer who does), these men can be treated with more attention at Temptations. Although they may not have money for Conquest, and as a result are not viewed as desirable, they are at Temptations, and if they are White, they have the symbolic capital associated with being White (i.e., it is assumed they have money).

Temptations tries to set itself apart from other New York strip clubs by being a gentleman's cabaret. According to its Web site, it is the "largest and newest upscale gentlemen's cabaret" in New York. Temptations promotes fine wine, gourmet food (lamb chops and seafood), champagne, beautiful dancers, large dressing rooms, and private showers and bathrooms for the dancers. It also provides a virtual tour of the club consisting of 55 photos of the club (front entrance, bar, and stage). The last line of the home page reads: "You will discover that Temptations is different from all the rest." In this ad, the club's promoters are classifying Temptations within a certain male customer milieu that values sophistication, but is out of sync with the area's greasy diners and fast-food restaurants that don't sell gourmet food. I have seen ads for Temptations in the *New York Post*,[14] but when I have seen men in Times Square promoting other strip clubs, they were wearing signs imprinted with the club's name, or passing out flyers, and were usually making minimum wage, which underscores a disconnect between the club's image and the reality of worker exploitation.[15]

Food and Cultural Capital at Conquest

Pierre Bourdieu (2002) classifies bourgeois meals as lacking taste for the heavy and fatty foods associated with the working-class meal. He states the following when observing food consumption among professional individuals:

The taste of the professionals or senior executives defines the popular taste, by negation, as the taste for the heavy, the fat and the course, by tending towards the light, the refined and the delicate. The disappearance of economic constraints is accompanied by a strengthening of the social censorships, which forbid coarseness and fatness, in favour of slimness and distinction. The taste for rare, aristocratic foods points to a traditional cuisines, rich in expensive or rare products. (p. 185)

This middle-class catering also implies that the club is classy, which can symbolize a geographic space shaped by class-based male desire. The menu at Conquest contains soups and salads (Caesar, house, warm goat cheese and spinach, buffalo mozzarella and tomato, and grilled prime sirloin steak salad). Appetizers consisted of shrimp cocktail, Maryland lump crab cakes, oysters on the half shell, fried calamari, and caviar; entrees are sirloin steak (16 oz), filet mignon, porterhouse, rib eye cop, rack of lamb, Kobe steak, half roasted free-range chicken, and grilled double chicken breast. Seafood fare is steamed Maine lobster and Maryland crab cakes. Similar to Temptations, the Conquest menu features soups, salads, steaks, chicken, and seafood. However, unlike Temptations, Conquest has foods that cater more to a middle-class and possibly health-conscious clientele (caviar, free-range chicken, oysters, and lobster).

Although customers at Conquest may be served hefty portions of food, which supports the notion of abundance being with the working-class meal, health-conscious food choices such as free-range chicken is often associated with a bourgeois lifestyle, in which people have the money to buy costly organic food.[16] Also, foods such as caviar, oysters, and lobster are connected to a middle-class lifestyle and taste for exotic dishes (Bourdieu, 2002). Both clubs aim for this effect, but in the case of Temptations this status may be viewed as being more an achieved status, whereas Conquest already has a reputation for being an upscale gentleman's club.

A dancer's erotic capital is affected by the larger environment of the club's location and thus club reputation, so if a club is deemed undesirable (i.e., by being in a low-income neighborhood with low property values), or undesirable based on club clientele, the status of the club is transferred onto the erotic capital of a dancer. Club status has consequences for how Black and Latina dancers are treated.

3

Race, Exchange, and Cultural Capital

White dancers can be a bit more direct in asking customers for money, whereas Black dancers will be seen as gold diggers and pushy.

—Natasha (24-year-old Black waitress at Conquest)

Pierre Bourdieu's concepts of habitus and fields are useful in understanding the various exchanges that occur among dancers and customers regarding space and desire and how erotic capital is used in these spaces of exchange. Jenkins (2002), describes Bourdieu's definition of a field as "a social arena in which people manoeuvre and struggle in pursuit of desirable resources" (p. 84). Desire industries, such as strip clubs, can be viewed as fields where individuals struggle to accrue resources, while cultural and erotic capital is exchanged between dancers, workers, and customers. Dancers and workers gain monetary/cultural capital within social networks, while customers gain social rewards, such as validation of their masculinity, social bonding with friends, and a feeling of helping the dancers economically.[1]

There also are codes of behavior that occur within strip clubs. These are similar to Bourdieu's (2001) definition of *habitus* as an unconscious set of dispositions "inseparable from the structures that produce and reproduce them, in both men and women" (p. 42). However, I believe the notion of the habitus also can be a conscious and racialized state of mind. For example, male customers may enter certain clubs because they feel the symbolic capital of the women who work there is less, and therefore they demand less money for services. These customers may act disrespectfully because they feel they can, which in turn can be an act of symbolic violence against the dancer. I view symbolic violence in desire industries as a form of violence normalized within the culture of some clubs to produce a lower erotic capital value among Black women, especially clubs, such as Temptations, that hire mostly Black and Latina women, and where the *visual* erotic capital of Black and Latina women is desired (i.e., larger bodies, darker skin), but the *economic* exchange value for their erotic capital is low.

In the case of predominately Black clubs, such as Temptations, structural neighborhood violence can explain the behavior toward Black dancers in these spaces, where police brutality, lack of economic resources, and Black-on-Black crime can become internalized by many inner-city Black and Latino male (and female) customers, and thus be revealed in their treatment of dancers and toward other customers.

These groups (in this case dancers and customers) exhibit their own individual habitus through the field of desire industries. For example, dancers perform their habitus by marketing their erotic capital via dancing on stage, giving lap dances in the VIP room, and performing various types of emotional labor, such as talking to customers, smiling, and appearing interested in their lives; masseuses walk up to customers offering them massages and engaging in conservation with them by smiling, making eye-contact, and appearing interested in their lives; waitress do the same; and male customers watch the dancers or walk up to the stage with money to tip them.

Crossing Racial Boundaries

I returned to Conquest to conduct field research and interview people at the site. A Latina woman I had asked to interview checked my bag, and gave me her e-mail address; she reached in her purse for a pen, and opened her wallet to show me a picture of her 4-year-old son. Next to the photo I noticed a white EBT card.[2] I found this significant because it signifies that she is working class and receiving public assistance, unlike many of the dancers at Conquest. A few minutes later while sitting at the bar I met Patrick, a young, White, Citigroup financial advisor. I asked him what he likes about Conquest. I learned he was 25 and in a long-term relationship with an Asian woman who is an artist. I asked him why he likes this particular club, as well as what kind of dancer he likes:

> I like Conquest because the women look attractive and confident. They smile and I like that because I find the face the most attractive part of a woman. I am often with a group of friends and my girlfriend, but sometimes I go alone, she doesn't know that, though. I am pretty open. I do find the Latina women to be friendlier than many of the White dancers.

When I asked Patrick if he had any views on Black women, he said that he found them to be socially aggressive. He said he never dated a Black woman and had few Black friends, but based his opinions on the Black women who worked as administrative assistants at Citigroup. He said, "The Black women who I work with are aggressive and very opinionated. At least that is the impression I get."

While we talked I pointed out a light-skinned Black dancer who was walking next to the stage asking men if they wanted a lap dance. I commented that she is pretty. Patrick looked at her and expressed that even though she was pretty, he hadn't noticed her before I pointed her out.

I write in my fieldnotes that it is worth noting that Patrick finds Black women aggressive, and yet they occupy one of the lowest ranks in his workplace and are invisible to him at Conquest, despite there being only a few women of color, resulting in Black women standing out.[3] The fact that Patrick didn't notice the Black dancer amid the White dancers underscores the hypersexuality of Black women, and how this corresponds to low erotic capital and social exchanges in desire industries.

Exchanges and Social Networks at Conquest

Based on its reputation for well-off customers, Conquest seemed to many of the workers who were not dancers a good place to network and exchange information. While sitting at the bar one night, I looked up to see a short, Middle Eastern-looking man wearing a purple vest standing next to me. He asked me to pick a card. I laughed, both surprised and amused by his request. I picked a card and he shuffled the deck, and then pulled the card from under his sleeve. He was the club magician and performs every Saturday and also during the week. His name is Ian and he also works as a bartender at other dance clubs. When I asked him what he likes about Conquest he said, "They let me do my magic tricks here, whereas at the other clubs, I can't." Conquest provides him the chance to do what he loves: magic tricks.

Steven, a bouncer from Russia and an economics major at Baruch College, felt that Conquest was a good place for networking:

> I am studying economics and I want to be an accountant, since so many men from Wall Street come in, I feel I will be able to network with some of them for jobs when the time comes for me to graduate.

Jesse, a Black bouncer from Brooklyn, works as a bodyguard for celebrities in addition to working at Conquest. He says: "By working here and interacting with the customers, I get opportunities for other jobs doing security." Melissa, a Puerto Rican who works the coat check, is studying hotel management, and feels her experience working in a customer service position at Conquest will prepare her for a career in the field. Monique, a Black dancer and student at the Fashion Institute of Technology, is interested in fashion design and models. She said she sometimes meets customers who do portfolios for free; however, she commented that many customers also want sex in exchange for their help. Jake, a co-owner from Staten Island, said these examples illustrate the high level of social exchange and networking that takes place at Conquest.

Erotic Capital and Exchange in Black Space

A consistent theme among Black dancers in my research was their negative experiences in all-Black male–female strip clubs; most said they would not work at an all-Black club if they didn't have to. Alicia, a 24-year-old Black Conquest dancer from Toronto, remembered her experiences working at a Black working-class strip club in Atlanta:

> I would never work at a Black strip club again. I worked once at a club in Atlanta, and the customers acted like they were just entitled to have you. They were rude; touched you even after you told them certain areas were off limits. Also, I remember I was charging $25 for a lap dance, and come to find out the actual price was $5, so I had other dancers getting mad at me because I was over charging. I quit after a few months there.

Natasha had worked as a hostess at the club FlashDancers in Times Square and also has worked as a bartender. She is 24, part U.S. Black and Ghanaian, has her own apartment in Crown Heights, and is currently a student at New York City Tech, but wants to transfer to Medgar Evers College for a bachelor's degree in psychology. Although she said she had worked at an all-Black club, she said she would not do it again:

> In the Black clubs there is no respect and the owners just want to try and get with you. I worked at Sugar Hill [a restaurant club] as a waitress from 1999 to 2003, and often the Black customers would not want to tip you. The Black men would always try and get with you, they weren't trying to look out for you or help you out. But the White men did. For example, a White bouncer told me about jobs out at Harbor Beach and the Hamptons.

According to Natasha, the Black men with whom she worked were not trying to help her gain resources for better jobs or increase her social and cultural capital, however, the White bouncers did. I interpreted this to signify the gender tensions between many Black men and women, and the internalization of Black women's hypersexuality by some Black men. Furthermore, some Black men feel that Black women are treated better than they are in the larger society, thus Black men may withhold information that would help Black women get ahead. White men, however, may appear more forthcoming with information largely because they often don't view Black women as a threat to their economic advancement the way some Black men might.[4]

However, Natasha said she wasn't always treated well at the White establishments where she worked. When she worked at the Fashion Café in Park Slope she made $300 a night as a bartender and $98 in tips. She was told by the manager that she was making too much in tips and eventually was fired—yet, despite this treatment she still preferred predominately White clubs.

Ideas of hypersexualization affect women differently. Lighter-skinned Black and mixed-raced women perform less work for tips, are touched less, and are desired more, by White and Black customers, whereas darker-skinned women work more for tips, are touched more, and are desired less by White and Black customers alike.

Getting More for Less:
Undervaluing of the Black Female Body

Hypersexualization of Black and Latina women also plays an important role in why some White men prefer predominately Black and/or Latina clubs such as Temptations. During a visit to Temptations, I observed two middle-aged White men dressed in suits sitting at the bar talking with two Latina dancers. Not only did I overhear them flirting, but I could hear one dancer trying to obtain some information regarding her taxes, thus I learned that the men worked in the financial industry. When the dancers left with one of the men for a lap dance, I took the opportunity to chat with the man still sitting at the bar. His name was Joseph, he was a 45-year-old from upstate New York. When asked why he likes Temptations he responded as follows:

> Honestly, I like coming here because you can touch more; at Conquest you can't touch. I also think Black women are sexy. Sometimes I am the only White man in here, especially at night when the hip-hop crowd with the baggy paints comes in; but I don't mind it. The women are not stuck up here like those White bitches at Conquest.

Joseph's response highlights the low erotic capital associated with Black clubs and Black women's bodies; his response also is consistent with what other interviewees said regarding the perception that Black clubs have lower standards than White clubs concerning touching and other forms of sexual contact. His comments also place White women as not cooperating with White male sexist notions that White women are available for them to touch, placing them in the "stuck up" category, and Black women in the "more" (i.e., sexual) category. The fact that Joseph acknowledges that he often is the only White man in the space, and doesn't mind this fact, shows that men can cross racial boundaries to consume desire, and that White men act out their sexism more in Black spaces, while maintaining the appearance of being respectable in White clubs.

Cristina offered insight into the White businessmen who frequented Conquest. She felt they were rude and said the men felt a sense of entitlement toward getting performances from dancers:

> At Conquest on East 60th Street the customers are older; at the one in Chelsea, the guys are younger. I think that is because it is new compared to the original one on East 60th Street, but overall customers tend to be arrogant. Businessmen are the worst; they feel the world should just cater to them.

During a conversation with Patrick at Conquest, the DJ played a rap song by Dr. Dre and I took this opportunity to ask Patrick about his thoughts on and whether he listened to gangsta rap. He smiled and replied that he did listen to it:

> I guess you could say that I feel more masculine listening to gangsta rap and going to Conquest. . . . I don't really see myself as masculine, and didn't date much in high school. I think there is a fantasy that is fulfilled for me here, but I would not date anyone from here; they are not my type.

For Patrick, the world of gangsta rap remains one of fantasy that is totally disconnected from his everyday reality as a middle-class White male. However, as the following interviews with Black and Latina dancers and customers show, the culture described in gangsta rap is anything but pure fantasy and is not removed from the everyday lives of Black/Latina dancers, workers, and customers.

Low Erotic Capital and Negative Exchange Value

The devaluing of Black women's bodies within desire markets reflects their low erotic capital in both sex and nonsex clubs (i.e., the fact that some of these women at nonsex clubs would sleep with someone for a drink versus some other material gain, such as a job or apartment). It also means that men who go to Black clubs (strip and regular clubs) feel more desirable as customers than they do at predominately White clubs largely because the unique exploitation of Black women's erotic capital leads them to feel as if they can get more sexual services for less.

During my fieldwork at Conquest, I met Edward, a 42-year-old Black man, who owns a limousine company. He picks up many customers from Conquest, and when he learned of my research project he was delighted to talk to me about his experiences being a customer of strip clubs that cater to a Black clientele and also of picking up customers from Conquest:

> The talent is better [at a predominately Black club] and the prices are cheaper than a place like Conquest, you get more for your money. At Conquest the dancers will charge you for everything, the drinks are expensive... at a lot of the Black clubs it ain't like that. The only thing I don't like is that you sometimes get a lot of thugs that go to these places, especially in New Jersey, where a lot of these clubs are located. When you go to a regular club, some Black women will have sex with a guy if he buys her a drink... why pay for it in a strip club when you can get it for free?

Natasha further elaborated on this point when she said, "You have some women who basically prostitute themselves in the [regular] clubs. Like a guy might buy them a drink and they give him a blowjob."

Both Edward and Natasha note the ways Black women occupy a space of low erotic capital in the sex industry and in the heterosexual dating market. At Black strip clubs one can get more (read: sexualized exchanges and drinks) for less money, which corresponds with the notion that Black women's bodies (and their labor) are worth less than White women's bodies and labor. This ranking reflects not only how Black women's bodies are exchanged in the sex industry, but also outside of it, where some men feel that they don't have to do much for a woman to have sex with them in these venues.[5]

However, according to Edward, Black strip clubs attract a less desirable client base compared with clubs such as Conquest. Regarding exchanges between the dancer and customer, Edward acknowledged that Black women do benefit from material exchanges with customers, but that White women get more from White men in terms of money. However, based on Edward's encounter with White customers, Black dancers are able to cross racial boundaries and market/exchange their erotic capital for material capital (i.e., have customers get apartments for them). As a customer, he often feels he is helping Black dancers because most of them have children: "There aren't a lot of Black dancers who don't have kids; most do. So, I know I am helping them out when I tip them and pay for lap dances."

Mike, a 29-year-old Black male, who works in construction, also felt that he was helping the dancers economically:

> A lot of my female friends say I am a misogynist because I go to strip clubs. But over the years I really get to know the dancers. I may, on a good night, spend about a $1,000. If I don't have money, I will bring a group of guys who do.

Edward and Mike feel they add to the social profit of dancers when they give them more than they had possessed prior to meeting them; in this case economic capital; however, for Patrick tipping was not a form of service, but mandatory:

> I feel tipping is mandatory; that often one doesn't have a choice. I am not good with telling a dancer if I feel overcharged for something, like a drink. So, I will just end up tipping even though I already spent a good deal of money.

In contrast to Edward and Mike, Patrick views tipping as a mandatory part of the experience and as something dancers expect of the customer. Patrick tips even if he feels the club (e.g., the drinks) are overpriced. When I asked Patrick if he thought any of these women were the stereotype of a "gold digger," he said, "When I think of a gold digger I think of a White woman with money who is trying to use a man for his money."

However, Natasha believes that White women can get what they want out of sexual relationships with men regarding material items, whereas when Black women do the same they are labeled gold diggers. This clearly expresses the low exchange value of Black women's bodies and the stereotype of working-class Black women taking advantage of government programs, such as welfare (Collins, 2004; Quadagno, 1996; Roberts, 1997).

I asked Natasha more about how her perception of Black women as gold diggers affects them as workers in industries of desire:

> I hear customers say that about some Black dancers at Flash-Dancers and at Sugar Hill there was that image of the pushy Black woman asking for money. Men come in the clubs and

think they will get a rap video with Black women all over them. White women will get what they want out of a relationship, like money, and they will not have to give up a lot. Black women who do the same thing are seen as gold diggers.

Natasha's racial view on the term *gold digger* differs from Patrick's because, although he associated the term with a sexist stereotype of a White woman out to get a rich White man's money, Natasha is perceptive enough to see that it often is a euphemism frequently used by Black men in rap songs to describe Black women. Also, although the term does not prevent White dancers from making money, it does stop Black and Latina women from being able to do so to the same degree as their White counterparts.

Black Bodies and Symbolic Representation

Natasha's analysis of erotic capital and crossing racial boundaries were largely negative based on her experience working as a bartender at a New York club, as well as on her dating experiences. The hypersexualization of Black women via music videos helps perpetuate the image of Black women as overly available sexually. Unlike Patrick's perception that rap videos were purely fantasy, they do have a direct effect on the well-being of Black women, especially those working in desire industries.

Natasha's views of not being supported by Black male customers or her co-workers, and the disrespect she felt when working at Black strip clubs, show that Black women have a lower erotic value to White and Black men. This low erotic value is tied to structural racism, sexism, and classism, as Natasha's work and neighborhood experiences show, and serve as a prelude to her experience within desire industries.

Trading in Capital: Exchanging Erotic for Cultural Capital

While observing customer relations with dancers, I asked dancers to describe some of the exchanges they receive from customer interactions besides monetary benefits. Most of the dancers said they didn't really get a lot, and most agreed that one must be leery of customers who promise to connect them with resources because often they just want to have sex with the dancers. Sonya, a 24-year-old Black dancer at Temptations and a graduate of Penn State, responded that some women are into drugs and exchange sex for drugs. Josie, a Latina who works as a waitress and is studying to be a nurse at Borough of Manhattan Community College, said that sometimes she meets chiropractors who give her discounts if she uses their services. Sonya said she enjoys the exchange of attention customers give her. "I always had a fantasy of being an actress or a singer, some kind of entertainer—that didn't happen, so what else will give you that feeling? Stripping." Besides the tax information that one White customer was exchanging with a Latina dancer when I observed at Temptations, most of the women viewed the job as a means to an end: a degree or an income. Many dancers felt customers wanted to sleep with them in exchange for their help, so they don't always take customers up on their offers of help. However, some women are able to have a lucrative exchange between erotic and cultural capital.

I met Cristina in a coffee shop on East 60th Street after weeks of trying to contact her by cell phone. Cristina is working on a master's degree in political science at Hunter College, and works at Conquest on East 61st to support herself while in school. She is a 24-year-old Puerto Rican from Spanish Harlem. She had just returned from a trip to Switzerland. She has had successful exchanges for her erotic capital with customers:

> There is this older Jewish man who is really nice and he helps me with my rent. I live on the Upper West Side where my rent is $1,550 [per month]. He sometimes helps me out with part of it, but a couple of times he has paid my full rent for me. He also helps me with my English, which is great. Like, if I mispronounce a word he will correct my English. He speaks perfect Standard English, so I feel like when he corrects me that helps me to speak better in school.[6] I pretend to care about what's going on inside of him. You have to pretend, you know? You have to act like you care about them. That's how you get regulars and sometimes they do things for you.

Cristina's description of this customer–dancer interaction supports the theory of emotional labor. Thus, according to Cristina, dancers have to pretend to like the customers in exchange for monetary value and, as I explore in the following sections, cultural capital.

Therefore, this customer helps Cristina with her English, giving her the linguistic capital necessary to succeed in college. In addition, he helps her pay rent so she can maintain a comfortable lifestyle in a desirable neighborhood. In exchange, she sometimes accompanies him on dinner dates. However, Cristina does not lose sight of the power he exercises in this relationship and the motives he may have for helping her (such as the possibility of sleeping with her). She stresses the importance of never having sex with the customers as a way to ensure that she is getting what she needs from the relationship while maintaining clear boundaries:

> Yes, I mean obviously he is getting something from the deal, also—power. I feel like they help you if they feel they have power over you, but the trick is to never sleep with them. I have learned how to be a bitch in this industry. I am book smart, but I am also street smart. You make them feel useful, and they feel good that they are helping you because it gives them a sense of power. They like a little tease, a challenge. If you are too easy you don't get what you want. You pretend to care about them, and they like you as long as you are also below them. I feel like in many ways they [the customers] want to keep you down.

Cristina's analysis of the power motives behind this customer's efforts to help her underscore the theory that not all social exchanges are done out of pure generosity, but sometimes to reinforce a superior status over the receiver of the exchange. Power is a theme that surfaces for Cristina regarding the customers and her view that they only help if they feel the dancers are beneath them, while simultaneously, dancers flirt with the customers, go out to dinner with them, but won't sleep with them. Patricia Hill Collins states that Black women hold "subjugated knowledge" designed to challenge the ideology of the dominant culture that oppresses them.[7] Cristina uses subjugated knowledge (pretending to be interested in the customers while understanding the power dynamics operating between her and the men) and her erotic capital to perform emotional labor to get what she wants from her customers, which she describes in the following comments:

> I sometimes meet this customer outside of the club. In exchange for dinner he may give me $400. I see this job helping me with my college education. I keep that as my main focus. Some women want trips and nice clothes from the customers. I have gone on trips, a customer helped me with my trip to Switzerland, but my main focus is school. I don't want to be in the industry forever, and I don't want to feel like I only have my looks going for me. I have a mind, too.

As this interview illustrates, Cristina is able to use her erotic capital to obtain monetary and culture capital, such as having someone help her with her English skills while getting her college degree, or help with rent so she can maintain a lifestyle that otherwise would be difficult for her to obtain working a regular job and going to school. It also shows that she is not a victim and is very aware of the power relations between she and her White, male, middle-class customers, as well as the racial stratification of women of color in desire industries. Although Latinas, like Black women, are hypersexualized, which often provides them fewer gains from their erotic capital in desire industries, some Latinas, like Cristina, were able to market their race and sexuality, and advance in class status.

4

Same-Sex Desire

Race, Class, and Gender Performance

I like dancing for women because I feel like I am part of a community and they just enjoy the show; women usually come with their girlfriends, so it's like they are out for a show. Men often don't respect you when you dance, and they want you to work harder, like by putting objects in your vagina. I don't like that . . . I like to feel safe when I dance; I don't always feel safe dancing for men.

—Sandy (25-year-old Black lesbian dancer)

A 40-year-old Black, butch-identified lesbian in Oakland named Silky, started Girlielicious in 2003. Silky started her own production company, Butchlicious Entertainment in 1999, while working in the collections department of a social security office in the city of Richmond. Girlielicious functions as a talent show with Black women strippers performing erotic acts. Silky got interested in promoting events in the lesbian, gay, bisexual, and transgendered (LGBT) community of the East Bay after performing and lip-syncing in gay clubs in the East Bay.[1] She said there was a lack of places for LGBT Black people to go and the few that did exist closed because of violence from other LGBT Black people attending the club: "During that time there were not a lot of spaces for gay people, but the one club that was here for gay men got closed down because of violence."

When I asked Silky where she thought the source of violence in the community came from, she responded: "Drugs, jealously, stupid stuff." Thus, part of the violence experienced in Oakland's working-class LGBT community is in response to a lack of space in which these individuals can meet one another and fully express themselves. In addition to the internal violence within the clubs, and the overall lack of socializing venues, Silky said there was a lack of clubs geared toward lesbians. So, at Girlielicious she welcomes everyone (gay, straight, transgender, and bisexual), as indicated on a promotional flyer, which reads "For Women who Love Women and Their Open-Minded Friends."

I welcome everyone: gay, straight, transgendered, whatever. I noticed in San Francisco when I would go to clubs there were a lot of gay and trans men, but not a lot of women. I wanted to do something especially targeting women. I also open up my space for straight people who are open-minded.

Silky describes the lesbians, who come to the event as a mixture of different individuals regarding level of out-ness (many are still in the closet), and various classes (some are professionals, others are working class, still others are unemployed, and some are involved in drugs). However, within the social milieu of Girlielicious, these various women come together in hopes of finding community—a place where they feel comfortable being themselves and dressing in ways that express their gender identity. For example, Silky expressed the freedom of being able to dress in a manner that illustrates her gender expression (which is often to wear a pin-striped suit such as those associated with pimps and a cane), as opposed to how she dresses in her office job:

> In the office I have to dress in a conservative manner, slacks, and a blouse. Here I can wear my suits. I often shop in the men's department at Macy's to buy my clothes; at Girlielicious I can really be myself.

Thus, Girlielicious offers a safe space for women who dress in a gender-variant (or gender nonconforming) manner.[2] It also allows for visually identifiable LGBT Black women, especially butch-identified women, to express their gender without the threat of the male violence often found in predominately straight clubs.

Mignon Moore (2006) discusses the ways gender is expressed for many Black lesbians through their style of dress, especially within Black lesbian spaces. According to Moore's study of Black lesbian gender presentation in New York:

> Athletic jerseys and baggy jeans on women as they walk down 125th Street in Harlem or Flatbush Avenue in Brooklyn do not immediately mark them as lesbian, but reveal their membership in a gender display category once they step into a convention center or nightclub filled with black lesbians. (129)

Silky's attire can be read as an expression of her gender and her role as promoter and a woman in control. I asked Silky about her public persona in the club as a pimp[3] and what this role represents to her, especially given the sexist context of Black women being portrayed as "hos" in mainstream hip-hop videos:

> It's really not about being a pimp, but being classy. My father used to wear suits, so I am dressing like him, I don't completely dress like a pimp; I may wear jeans and a nice dress shirt with a tie, not the whole suit, and no jewelry. I also see it as flipping the image of the pimp from a man who controls women, to a woman who is not afraid to do her own thing with her body.

I later inquired about her marketing techniques and the flyers used to advertise Girlielicious. The flyers often feature Black women with their backs turned from the camera, thus highlighting their butts. I asked if she views this differently than how men market Black women in the porn and hip-hop industry. She states: "No, just that I cater to the lesbian/gay Black community; other than that, there is no difference."

My interview with Silky illustrates that lesbian marketing of erotic capital pertaining to Black women is not that different from heterosexual marketing, especially in hip-hop videos, which often highlight Black women's butts and overall curvy figures, along with long hair either braided or straightened.

However, one difference between the marketing of venues such as Girlielicious, and mainstream hip-hop videos, is that Black women's bodies are the subjects of desire for other Black women. Even though Girlielicious provides a venue for lesbian erotic capital to be performed and exchanged among Black women, and a community for queer Black women, one can argue that some of the gendered categories performed (such as that of the pimp and the ho) reproduces sexist and racist controlling images of Black femininity and masculinity that reinforce female subordination, even as women like Silky try to turn these meanings on their head as a form of empowerment.

Violence, Urban Space, and Erotic Capital

In October 2005, after conducting research at Girlielicious with a female friend, we walked past a group of teenaged Black boys who were heading toward downtown Oakland. As we passed them, one touched my rear, no doubt demonstrating his manhood in front of his peer group. I yelled at him and we proceeded to walk to our destination. Incidents of sexual harassment are, unfortunately, very commonplace for Black women residing in Oakland.

Racial and class segregation, along with police violence, augments intracommunity violence among Blacks in urban areas such as Oakland. This creates an environment in which people feel the need to inflict violence or they become victims of it. This has a dual impact on Oakland's Black LGBT communities, because both queer clubs and the overarching ghetto are two types of contained spaces where movement is confined to these spaces based on fear of violence and/or racial and economic restrictions. Historically, in order to survive Black people were forced to blend into the larger community and suppress differences to create a unified racial identity in response to White supremacy. White racism and de jure racial segregation made this necessary before the Civil Rights Movement. This was especially true for Black queer people who, in places such as Harlem, co-existed (although not always in harmony) with the larger straight Black community (Chauncey, 1994; Collins, 2004; Mumford, 1997).

However, as a result of integration, institutionalized racism, and consequently re-segregation, many queer Blacks live in the inner city with their straight counterparts and develop ways of blending into the larger community. Blending is often done as a means of avoiding homophobic harassment and violence, and also as a way to display group membership and preserve the love of their families and friends.

Therefore, Blacks as a group are hyper-segregated with a history of also being hypersexualized. The presence of queer Blacks in the ghetto connects these two categories not only because heterosexual Blacks are viewed as hypersexual, feeding into their marginalization as a result of stereotyping Black women as being on welfare or Black men as violent criminals, but Black queers are seen as hypersexual because of the stereotypes of both Black and queer people evolving around a deviant sexuality (Cohen, 1997; Collins, 2004).

In many ways, the connection among race, space, class, and sexuality in the segregated inner city of Oakland illustrates Max Weber's (1958) notion of ideal types pertaining to segregation of the ghetto, because the ideology of hypersexualization and hyper-segregation ensures that the ghetto stays marginalized. This is the environment where many of the women at Girlielicious live, and it shapes the erotic capital women hold, the violence between women in this community, along with the gender roles performed among the women.

Girlielicious honors key events in the women's lives, such as birthday events, anniversaries, and memorials of women who died in the East Bay as a result of inner-city violence. This was made evident during one of my trips when there was a memorial for a young Black woman who had attended Girlielicious events, and was murdered during a drive-by shooting in Oakland—she was an innocent bystander. A few of the women wore white T-shirts with the words "Stop the Violence" on the front. Silky requested a moment of silence in the club before the performance to acknowledge the loss. "Tomorrow is not promised," she reminded the audience as they bowed their heads in silence. After a few minutes, the DJ continued to play hip-hop and the crowd went back to dancing before the show began. This is an example of the many functions Girlielicious serves in Oakland's community of LGBT Black women—valuing the lives of LGBT Black women marginalized by sexuality, race, class, and gender.

This event also underscores the unique forms of violence faced by LGBT Black women. Unlike their White counterparts, these LGBT Black women deal with the kinds of violence that plague poor inner-city Blacks in general: drive-by-shootings and police brutality, as well as specific anti-LGBT violence. Therefore, Girlielicious provides a space for people to mourn loved ones lost to the epidemic of inner-city violence, a reality often not dealt with at mainstream White gay and lesbian venues in the Bay area.

The Performance of Erotic Capital for Women: Not Just Entertainment

Women who perform erotic labor emphasize the transgressive nature of women who perform as exotic dancers and break down the dichotomy between the public and private sphere, where sex is reserved for the private sphere. The performance of heterosexuality, especially concerning butch women transforming themselves via make-up, wigs, and costumes into feminine women, also has been written about (Nagle, 1997). The study of the performance of heterosexuality for women who are exotic dancers illustrates Judith Butler's (1990) theory that gender is performed along with heteronormativity (see also Delacoste & Alexander, 1987). However, most scholarship on women as exotic dancers focuses on women performing for men, even if queer women are present in these industries that appear exclusively heterosexual. So, queer/lesbian spaces for women to perform as exotic dancers for other women are important, not only for female-centered entrainment, but also as a way to provide a sense of community and/or as political spaces for women to gather. Leila Rupp and Verta Taylor (2003) studied drag shows in Key West and argue that these performances also are political events in which drag queens create and support their identities. I find a similar dynamic in spaces where female exotic dancers perform for women. For example, clubs such as Girlielicious are spaces for poor/working-class queer Blacks to be out and meet each other, unlike in their everyday lives, where many of them are closeted for fear of violence and/or of being ostracized within the larger community in which they live.

Many women who attend Girlielicious appreciate and acknowledge the fact that they have a space in which to meet and mingle. For example, C.K., a 26-year-old self-identified aggressive,[4] felt that Girlielicious was a good place to hang out, despite some random fights among the women:

> I like coming to Girlielicious because the music is good and it's just a good spot to hang out with my friends, even though fights break out sometime, I feel the positive outweighs the negative.

Latrice a 30-year-old butch woman felt it was a good place to be able to get away for a few hours:

> I like coming here because it's just a nice spot to get away, especially if you work 40 hours a week. This is a good place to come, have a drink, and chill with your friends. Also, the music is off the hook, so the music is good—it's just the place to be.

Wanda, a 45-year-old Black lesbian from East Oakland, felt that the violence undermined the possibility of community-building among Black lesbians, and supported Girlielicious because it provides a space for Black lesbians to come together, despite the violence, or what she called the "ghetto" behavior of some of the women:

> Some of the women just act crazy, bringing weapons in the club, drinking, and fighting. But I come to support the space and I like the performances, but sometimes people just act ghetto.

Hence, Girlielicious functions for many of the women as a Black lesbian space to gather with friends, dance, have a drink, and basically stay off the street. One way the women in my study blended in with the larger East Oakland community was by dressing like their straight counterparts: femmes dressing like straight women in their neighborhood, and butches/studs dressing like the men in their neighborhood. Thus, dress and gender presentation are important elements of identity formation and community membership for these women.

Dress and Gender Presentation at the Girlielicious

When I visited Girlielicious, I noticed that it is located near the straight Black clubs. There were young men catcalling to women outside of the club. There are a couple of restaurants, a Best Western Hotel, and a few clubs on the way to the Girlielicious; however, for the most part, downtown Oakland is pretty deserted and men in cars often slowed down to look at my friend and I as we walked to the club.

When we approached the club, we saw a line of masculine-looking Black women. There was a White woman at the front frisking people before letting them in; I also noticed a sign enforcing the dress code of no baggy jeans. The fact that we had to be frisked before entering seems to mirror not only the reality that this happens at the other clubs, but a larger issue of crime and policing in low-income Black communities.[5]

The dress code enforcing the rule of no baggy jeans also conveys what type of crowd is welcomed at the space; in this case a nonviolent crowd because baggy jeans are associated with poor/working-class hip-hop culture and violence. However, for women at Girlielicious the issue of violence and the association of certain attire (such as baseball caps, do-rags, and baggy jeans) with violence is cause for distinguishing between forms of gender-role performance and style (Moore, 2006).[6] Dress style also is a way of blending into the larger Black community to avoid violence. Many butch and femme Black, inner-city women dress in ways that mirror how working-class men and women dress in their community. So, butches often wear Timberlands, baseball caps, gold chains, and sport gold teeth; femmes will sometimes wear long weaves, fake fingernails, chains with their name in gold, and Baby Phat[7] clothing. Some may be out as queer in the club, but remain closeted in their work and home lives.

Once inside, we were greeted by a Black woman dressed in a dress shirt and slacks. She appeared to be in her late 40s to early 50s. As we walked around, I noticed tables of masculine-looking Black women. I actually couldn't tell if some were women or men until I heard them speak—some also may have been transgendered men. There were a few men in the club, but they tried to not draw attention to themselves; they just sat quietly watching the women dance with each other. The environment has a prom aesthetic with balloons and glitter on a white-covered table. I was amazed by the number of butch and femme, mostly Black couples on the dance floor. One femme woman was wearing a T-shirt that read: "How do you know what your man wants?" as she grinds up against a butch looking woman. The femmes were wearing mini skirts, and heels, whereas the butches sported pin-striped suits, some had on the pimp attire complete with a cane. A woman named Donna stood out because she was wearing a pink suit with white pinstripes, pink suede shoes, shades, and had a bald head; she had a femme woman wearing a black dress on her arm.[8]

The emcee is a heavy-set Black butch woman who appears to be part Asian. She is dressed in a suit and carries a cane, as she tries to keep the audience hyped by preparing them for the upcoming featured dancer, "Goldie" from Atlanta. While waiting for Goldie to come on stage, Barbara, a masculine-looking Black woman in her late 30s, approached me on the dance floor. I used this as an opportunity to ask about her interest in the venue. She explained it was her first time at the club, and said she had heard about it through word of mouth. Barbara is from East Oakland, a mother of two sons, one of whom is a student at Monterey State and a Costco employee. I asked her what kind of women are attractive to her to so I could gain a sense of the erotic capital that is valued in the space. She said, "I like thin women. They could be thick [meaning curvy], but I don't like them too big."

Like many women at Girlielicous, Barbara is working class and presents in a masculine fashion. She associates thinness with being attractive, which can be interpreted as her reinforcing traditional gender roles because she dates femme women; thus there is an expectation that the femme is thin.

Susan Bordo (1993) examines the role of thinness in communities that were historically seen as accepting of larger size women, but now have joined the mainstream regarding desiring women to be thin. She states that the following:

> Unmuscled heft is no longer acceptable as it once has in lesbian communities . . . in the nineties, features on diet, exercise, and body-image problems have grown increasing prominent in maga- zines aimed at African American readers, reflecting the cultural reality that for most women today—whatever their racial or ethnic identity, and increasingly across class and sexual-orienta- tion differences—free and easy relations with food to be a relic of the past. (p. 103)

At Girlielicious, this dynamic of body size and traditional gender roles in a Black queer, female space is pronounced among many women identifying as both butch and femme.

When Goldie comes out on stage she is a beautiful curvy woman with long straight black hair. She was wearing a black corset with black leather boots. She danced to hip-hop music and did floor shows in which she crawled on the floor with her back to the audience while showing her butt. The emcee placed a bucket of water on stage as a prop, and Goldie slowly poured it on herself as the audience screamed and cheered her on. She then stripped down to a black bikini—her show is erotic and entertaining, a celebration of Black women's bodies and erotic capital.

Performing and Erotic Exchange Between Women

I later meet a young Black woman named Spice who has been dancing in both male and female venues since she was 16 and who identifies as a lesbian, but markets herself as bisexual within the erotic dancing industry (more about this is explored within the interview). She is a student at a junior college in San Francisco and hopes to promote her own club venue where women can perform. I met Spice in a café on Haight Street in San Francisco, and she showed up energetic, wearing a sweat suit. She is 5'5", has an olive complication, and dyed blonde curly hair. I asked her how she was introduced to dancing and about her educational and employment experiences. She explained:

> I have been working ever since I was 14. I used to work at McDonald's making $1,400 a month. I moved out at 15 and got my own apartment because my parents were into drugs. While working at McDonald's I met an older woman who was about 27 through a mutual friend, and she suggested I work in a strip club. So, I got a fake ID and started dancing.

Spice viewed working at McDonald's as respectable and is proud that she started working at a young age to support herself through high school:

> I went to an alternative high school in Vallejo, where they allowed me to do my work from home. I was home-schooled for part of my education, so this felt normal to me. I felt different from other students since I was already working and had my own apartment.

When I asked about dancing as opposed to working at McDonald's, she replied:

> I thought it was better than McDonald's. I made in a night what I made in a week there. My mentor also taught me the rules to dancing. She always told me to get my money upfront before I start dancing for any customers, so I don't get shortchanged later.

I then asked her about the types of exchanges she had experienced with customers she had experienced, and whether she ever sees customers outside of the club:

> [Spice hesitates to answer the question] "Yeah, sometimes . . . but it's all on my own terms. Sometimes I may have dinner with them, but only the ones who have real money, like an investor, someone like that. They range from everything: rich, poor, all ages and races. But yeah, some help me with my finances. One guy is in the stock market and he lets me see his account and

what he invests in to help me learn the stock market. This is
good since I am interested in investing and eventually having
my own business. I feel safe with the audience. I think most
of the drama is between the people dating each other, not
the performers.[9]

Similar to Cristina, who received benefits from exchanges with customers, Spice receives benefits from exchanges that go beyond monetary value,
such as knowledge that can help her become financially independent. She
also interacts with different types of customers, ranging from politicians and
investors to working-class men of various races and ethnicities. Spice also
had experiences dancing in a variety of clubs, straight and lesbian, in the
Bay Area, as well as venues that predominantly employ women of color as
dancers.

Spice has danced at many lesbian venues in Oakland and has worked
in music videos making $75 an hour. She also has danced at a few "straight"
Black clubs, where she felt management was trying to get "something for
nothing" and the women weren't valued. I asked her if there are any differences between dancing in "straight" versus queer clubs. She responds:

> I like dancing for women because the space allows for more
> creativity and theatrical performances and costumes. I also design
> clothes, and want to start my own clothing line, so I like design-
> ing my own costumes. The money is good. I often make about
> $150 to $350 a night.

Another difference Spice observes is that women managers are different
than male managers and often tend to be not as professional:

> They [female managers] may hire someone who is out of shape
> for example. You could be 300 pounds, but look tight, but they
> may hire someone totally out of shape because they want to give
> everyone a chance to perform, or they feel sorry for the woman.
> They lose sight that this is a business. Sometimes they may be
> disorganized or there is a lot of miscommunication, whereas in
> male clubs there is a lot of competition among the women, but
> they are aware this is a business. Also, women have guilt some-
> times about using each other as resources and networking . . . they
> need to learn how to use people for information.

However, Silky feels that it is important for her to give everyone a
chance to perform:

I give everyone a chance to perform. Many dancers are working mothers who work 9 to 5. I give everyone an opportunity
to perform and make some money; single mothers often need
additional money.

According to Spice, the level of attractiveness of dancers in women's
clubs is lower than at male clubs, but everyone is given a chance to market
and perform their erotic capital in the women's clubs. Spice feels that women
managers are not as business savvy as men, even though male mangers are
viewed as taking advantage of dancers by charging them high stage fees, and
by not making their well-being and safety a priority. In contrast Silky, like
some of the male customers I interviewed, views herself as helping the dancers
by providing them a space in which to perform and earn extra money. This
is significant because many of these women might not be hired anywhere
else based on weight restrictions at other clubs. Even if they were hired at a
lower-tier male-managed club with flexible standards, the work environment
may not be safe concerning harassment from male customers.

Sandy, a 25-year-old Black dancer I met in Hayward but who lives in
Richmond, is trained as a hip-hop dancer and performs at lesbian venues
in the Bay Area where she receives exposure for her dancing. Performing at
these venues helps her obtain opportunities to perform and/or do promotions
for parties in the Oakland queer community and thus make extra money.
She felt that performance of Black erotic capital is not as appreciated at the
White clubs as it is in Black clubs:

At many White clubs they don't like dancers to do booty claps
or tricks with your butt, but at the Black clubs, especially at the
male ones, they really like this.

Sandy and Spice both view performing for women as a way to help
them start their own businesses in some aspect of the entertainment industry,
and they feel a sense of community performing for women.

Racial Representation, Marketing,
and Erotic Capital at Girlielicious

I asked Spice about racial marketing when dancing. She said that she markets herself as whatever the customers want her to be, thus underscoring the
fluidity of racial categories, especially for mixed-race individuals.

I learned to be whatever they want me to be because they are
there for a fantasy. I remember I used to actually tell them what

I am [Black, Native American, and Scottish] and they would get turned off because that's not what they saw me as—they saw me as Latina or Black. If I were dancing for them at a table, they would not spend a lot of time with me. So, I learned to ask them what I looked like to them, and based on what they said, I would tell them that is my racial identity.

Spice's response speaks to her ability to pass between racial identities, although she clearly has African features. When I asked her about marketing techniques of club managers at Black and Latina clubs, she replied that they use old photos of White women from the 1970s to advertise dancers. Yet, at Girlielicious, Spice does not view these racial marketing techniques as occurring because the club is mainly Black and many of the women who work there fit within nontraditional standards of beauty (i.e., body type, skin color). However, Sandy views Spice as having more options for being on the cover of the flyers for Butchlicious events possibly because she is a light-skinned Black woman with blonde hair:

Even though I have danced longer than Spice, I feel she has first choice in terms of shifts, and photos shoots for the women's events. I am not sure why, but I feel it is because she is light-skinned with blonde hair.[10]

This statement underscores the fact that some non-White groups can pass as White versus other groups, such as Asians, Blacks, or dark-skinned Latino/as; it also displays how race is socially constructed and can shift depending on the category. It also illustrates the privileging of light skin and its correlation with higher levels of erotic capital in Black communities, including queer communities.[11]

Women Promoters, Femme Dancers, and Masculine Audiences

A week after my interview with Spice I returned to Girlielicious with a friend. When we arrived at the entrance we were frisked by a female security guard, and after showing our identification, we paid our $10 cover charge. Once inside, we took a seat near the stage and listened to the sound of the late rapper, Notorious B.I.G. playing on the stereo. The layout of the club consists of a bar with two television screens displaying the news, a pool table near the entrance, 10 tables with sets of four chairs in the middle of the club, and the stage toward the front. It was 10 p.m. and I counted 22 people, among them one White man, a Black man whom I assumed was his boyfriend, and two Black women at a table across from us. The White man is dancing to the music and imitating Black hip-hop moves by gyrating his hips and occasionally grinding against the other man while the women laugh.

In my fieldnotes I wrote that he was one of four Whites in the space, the others were an older White man at the bar, a female bartender, and a middle-aged man. There were many Black butch women and fewer femmes, although more people were coming in. I noted that many different identities intersected in the space: femmes, butches, people wearing grills,[12] men dressed in hip-hop gear, and a transgender Black woman sitting at a table next to us. Judging from their dress styles and speech patterns, most people in the audience appeared to be from poor/working-class backgrounds. Silky, was at the bar wearing her trademark attire: a purple and white pimp suit complete with a cane and hat.

The lights dimmed and the show was about to start. The host, a heavy-set Black woman named Lady Lana, came on stage and welcomed the audience. Once the audience finished clapping she announced that there would be no bullshit, and that there are two rules: no drugs or violence, and no sex. She then stated that everyone must give the performers respect, and that if anyone was interested in performing they must have good hygiene and be attractive—people in the audience laugh. I wrote in my fieldnotes that the rules reflected the frisking at the door and the heavy police presence in Oakland, where actions of patrons are regulated and security is strongly enforced, while simultaneously fights break out and sometimes weapons are brought in.

The performances are scheduled like a talent show, and there are 10 performers. Many of the women have elaborate outfits consisting of silver and other colorful revealing dresses, with shoes just as stylish. They market their erotic capital by performing on stage to a song, and walking around interacting with audience members for tips; common forms of interaction are lap dancing. One thing I notice is the explicit nature of many of the performances; one woman let someone suck on her breast during a lap dance for $1, another woman pulled pearls out of her vagina, providing the audience lots of shock value as people stood up in their chairs to see her performance. Spice critiqued what she felt were women giving away too much for too little money:

> I don't like it, and I don't think the audience does, either. Women who do that may have shock value, but if you watch closely, they don't get any money for it.[13] It just brings down the standard for the rest of us. It is also the result of the newer dancers not having proper mentoring into the industry and not knowing what

prices they should charge for services—that should be a private show, not public. Also, when they do that, they put the venue at risk for losing its liquor license.

Barbara also was critical of acts that involved dancers putting objects (such as beer bottles) inside of their bodies as part of their performance: "I don't like that. I don't think it is sexy, but some women do. Some women even have sex like that. I don't."

Sandy also disapproved of the sex acts that some dancers perform, feeling that most people want to see artsy performances that involve talent and skill. She said women who do those performances often do so for men where that type of performance is encouraged:

> Many women who do those tricks are used to dancing for men where they want us to stick things in ourselves, but women often think "isn't she going to get a yeast infection?"; whereas many men don't care. Also, because women dancers perform at the same venues for the same audience, that trick becomes boring because everyone saw the dancer pull pearls out of her pussy, but for the men they like it because they haven't seen the trick before.

However, Silky feels differently about these graphic performances:

> I think they [the dancers] are really into giving the audience a good show and getting the attention of the audience. I like when dancers are into their performance and use prompts with their shows. They sometimes make up to $300 on stage. I make my money from the cover at the door. I don't take a cut from dancers.

In this case, the dancer's erotic capital did not have high exchange value for graphic performances based on the low amount of tips she received from the audience for the act. Contrary to Silky's assertion that dancers could make this much in tips, I did not see evidence of this kind of money being generated for the dancers who performed the most graphic acts—I often saw dancers getting in total $20 (often in $1 bills) for these performances. The show ended with a church-like sermon by Lady Lana asking the audience to give thanks to God and asking God to bless them. I noted that this was an interesting intersection of religion and sex in a Black space as people joined her in saying "Amen" while exiting the venue. Spice is critical of this part of the show, feeling it isn't an authentic gesture from the women who run the space:

This is not a religious venue, I feel like there is something fake about the whole church thing . . . you know, just be yourself.

Silky thinks the audience likes it and feels comfortable:

A lot of Black people are brought up in the church, so in that way it is culturally familiar to them . . . especially being gay where many feel excluded from church; this is a way they can reclaim that.[14]

Given the multiple functions of the Black church, the historical significance of churches as sites of social activism among Black communities, and the unfortunate exclusion many queer Blacks feel within churches, it makes sense that cultural elements of the church are used in Black LGBT community-building—especially in a venue such as Girlielicious that offers exotic performances, which, like queerness, is viewed as immoral.[15]

Gender Trouble in the Ghetto

In *Gender Trouble: Feminism and the Subversion of Identity*, Butler (1990) explored the concept of gender as an unfixed category.[17] Influenced by Michel Foucault's concept of discourse and power relations, she argued that feminist discourse did not take into account the various identities affecting the category of "woman" such as race and class, and argued for a distinction between sex and gender. In *Undoing Gender*, Butler (2004) returns to the idea of complicating gender identities and examines notions of heterosexual normativity and a rejection of same-gender desire within the consolidation of gender norms:

I am trying to show how a prohibition on certain forms of love becomes installed as an ontological truth about the subject: The "am" of "I am a man" encodes the prohibition "I may not love a man," so that the ontological claim carries the force of prohibition itself. (p. 199)

However, what about butch and femme roles where individuals may be of the same sex (male/female) but different gender identifications (transgendered, butch, femme)? These hetero-normative roles are reproduced in queer communities so that the consolidation of gender norms may be "I am a femme, therefore I may not desire another femme" or "I am a butch, therefore I may not love a butch."

Butler describes the masculinity of the butch woman as "one not to be found in men" (p. 197). Although I agree with Butler that the category of the butch woman and the way masculinity is performed does not mirror that of men per se, I argue that in examining these roles within working-class Black queer spaces in Oakland, the masculinity of the butch/stud often mirrors that of the men in the community, and tells us something about the erotic capital and value of Black women's bodies (especially femme women) in those spaces. Variables such as class, neighborhood location, and gender presentation shape the relationships and erotic capital of queer Black women in the East Bay.

In the Black queer women's community of Oakland, gender roles often reflect larger gender relations of the communities in which many Black queer women live; this is especially true for the self-identified stud who crosses gender lines. At Girlielicious, I met Gail, a 26-year-old self-identified Black butch who is a student at San Francisco State University. I asked her what she thought about the gender dynamics between butch/studs and femmes in the community. She said she felt they mirrored Black heterosexual gender relations with regard to racism:

> I feel that the Black butch/stud is sort of treated like Black men in the larger society, in terms of feeling like it's harder for them to get jobs, or that they experience more racism from Whites than femmes do, so they might take their frustrations out on the femme.

Nekia, a Black woman in her mid-20s who dated butch women, feels that butches are insecure with their masculinity when compared with men, especially when men try and hit on their femme girlfriends in their presence:

> I know that the butches I have dated are intimidated by men, especially when they flirt with me and feel that this wouldn't happen if they were men.

Mark, who works as a bouncer for Studlicous events, feels that inner-city butch women model their masculinity after men who perform a thuggish style of masculinity, especially in their manner of dress (baseball caps, baggy pants) and attitude:

> Some women, especially the younger crowd, model their behavior after rappers like 50 Cent, and feel they have to be hard to gain respect of the men, but men usually don't give them that respect and you have fights that can break out between them. When

that happens, the butch suddenly wants to say she is a woman and that she should be treated like one—I feel they [butches] try and play both sides of the field.[16]

C.K., a self-identified "aggressive," felt that men often viewed her masculine presentation as a threat to their own masculinity:

I don't know what it is but men feel threatened by me especially when I am with my girlfriend. I guess they feel like, "How she get her?" So, I feel like I gotta be hard just to walk down the street.[17]

Sandy feels that violence between butches and femmes erupts around relationship dynamics, and that butches sometimes handle encounters the way some men in the community do: by extreme violence or force.

A couple of weeks ago at Girlielicious at the end of the show, a butch woman got into an argument with her girlfriend because she felt her girlfriend was cheating on her at the club. She pulled out a gun and was going to shoot her; luckily security was there to handle it and escorted her out. She is banned from ever entering the club again. In lesbian clubs they don't always check you to see if you have a weapon; they figure if you are a regular, you cool. In the straight clubs they always frisk people for weapons no matter how often they see you.

When asked if butches were mostly the ones who injected violence in relationships, many respondents stated that femmes also were violent, often in their relationships with butch/stud women. Silky felt that femmes could be just as violent as the butches:

My experience is that the femmes are violent. I dated a woman once who tried to hit me. I don't hit women unless it's self-defense . . . she was on drugs. There is a lot of insecurity . . . many femmes don't want their butch girlfriends to come to Girlielicious and look at other women. In dating relationships, many people have trust issues, like they think their partner is cheating on them, or drug problems.

Mark also felt femmes could be violent:

It's not always the butches, often we have to escort the femmes from the clubs because they are jealous of someone or some other relationship issue.

Sandy had a violent encounter with a butch girlfriend:

> I broke my ex-girlfriend's car window one night in front of Girlielicious. She accused me of cheating on her, which I wasn't, and she hit me from behind on my head, so I turned around and busted out her windows. I know that was crazy [laughing] but I had to defend myself and save face—I didn't want her to think she could get away with hitting me.

Many of the women I interviewed were perpetrators and/or survivors of violence. Like many working-class Black queer women, they were dealing with multiple forms of oppression (race, class, gender, sexual orientation), not just a single marginal identity (Crenshaw, 1984; Lorde, 1984). As mentioned earlier, one of the reasons Silky went into promoting was because of the violence in the gay clubs; she wanted to create a safe venue for queer and straight people to gather. The testimonies of violence from queer Black women in Oakland challenges notions of a nonviolent community among lesbians and that the butch is the one who is violent (Girshick, 2002).

Negotiating Violence and Boundaries at the Club

In strip clubs, connections between Black women's erotic capital and violence emerges when considering how women are treated as performers by customers, and how dancers negotiate violence in the clubs they work in. Spice has worked at a number of Déjà vu clubs in San Francisco, known for their ill treatment of dancers via the payment of stage fees and low-level security. She experienced violence at these clubs:

> The managers didn't deal with violence toward the dancer. You don't just wait for security if you want to survive; you've got to handle it yourself. I used to hit the customers with this big metal purse I would carry on stage that had my make-up in it, but I would carry it to hit the customers if they tried to hit me or touch me in the wrong way. Once this White frat boy type came in and thought he was going to get a free dance. I told him a dance was $20, and he kept trying to bargain me down. I was on stage getting ready to walk over to another customer, and he grabbed my arm. I told him to stop, but he wouldn't let go, so I hit him over the head with my purse. The manager was angry that I was hitting customers, but I told him, "you can't expect me to put up with that shit if you're not doing anything

about it." They [managers] also hired short nonthreatening men as security. If you want to have customers behaving appropriately, you have to have the idea of intimidation to make people fear doing something wrong in the club.

Sandy felt dancing for men was more dangerous than performing for women, even with the sporadic violent climate of the women's clubs:

Men want to touch you and are often aggressive and don't want to pay the price you want. They also show off in front of their friends and may refer to you as a bitch or a ho, you just never know what can happen, especially at a bachelor party where you don't even know if security will be there.

However, Mark feels that queer Black clubs can be just as violent as straight ones, attributing this to the marginalization of the former:

There are strikes against you for being gay, Black, and owning a club. I feel integration has a lot to do with some of the internal violence in both the straight and gay Black club scene, cause this doesn't happen in the White gay clubs. Now, because people can take their money somewhere else, there is a lack of respect because we don't have to go to Black clubs.

The lack of security and violence described by Spice, Mark, and Sandy speaks to the low erotic value of Black women's bodies when it comes to matters of safety. I asked Spice if, when dancing for men, she ever considered strip clubs that had the reputation of being more upscale, such as Mitchell Brother's in San Francisco, or the Lusty Lady, which is a co-op and unionized,[18] thus providing better working conditions. She replied that she auditioned for Mitchell Brother's and didn't get hired, but felt that she was making enough money at the other clubs, so she didn't mind. For Spice, economic stability was more important than the club's environment.[19]

According to Silky, one advantage that she offers is that she provides work for Black women dancers who otherwise would not be hired as exotic dancers. However, some would disagree that Silky is a good promoter; Sandy feels that Silky doesn't have the respect that a promoter should have:

Silky doesn't command respect; she always has to yell at people to get them to be quiet, whereas Lady Lana doesn't have to do that. People know what's up, and that if they act up, they are thrown out.

Despite the fact that Lady Lana is respected violent events among women do occur, as Sandy said. Spice feels that the femmes need to demand their rights and stand up against violence. "I identify as an aggressive femme; as femmes we need to stand up for ourselves." Thus, even in women's spaces there are issues of power and dominance that create dynamics similar to those in heterosexual spaces. The issue of violence and erotic capital in Black queer, female spaces is complicated by the marginalization of the women in these spaces on the basis of race and class.

This was illustrated during the end of my study when I witnessed a fight at Girlielicious. A friend of mine had warned me that there had been an incident a few months before in which someone had entered the club with a gun—the gun had passed through relaxed security. On the night I was there, a security guard frisked me and checked my bag for weapons. I asked him if people brought weapons into the venue, and his response, "not if I'm here," indicated that he was not as relaxed about security as some other guards might be. Once inside I was greeted by queer Black men who were attending an event prior to Girlielicious. They were middle-aged and from Oakland. I enjoyed watching them drink, laugh, and dance to the hip-hop and R&B music played by the DJ. Slowly, the men left and the women started coming in. I recognized many of the butch and femme couples from my time in the field. The TV screen displayed hip-hop videos featuring light-skinned Black women with long hair as a love interest. I wrote in my fieldnotes that the contrast between the women on the TV screen and the dancers could be a sign of protest because the dancers were diverse along the lines of sexuality, skin color, and body size. However, I also noted that some of these mainstream standards were reproduced within the stud/femme paradigm of erotic capital, where sometimes the femmes might resemble the women in the videos, and would be expected to perform to an erotic standard that butches might be exempt from.

An hour later, Lady Lana came out to give her usual welcome, including a warning that no negative behavior or fighting would be allowed. When she said this, a Black woman sitting next to me at the bar rolled her eyes and said, "She always says that." I agreed with her and waited for the performers to come on. The first performer was Sandy; she danced on stage and in the audience wearing a bright blue bikini—the women went wild tipping her with $1 bills. I later saw the security guard come in to make sure people were behaving properly. Suddenly, without warning, a group of people to the far left of the stage started fighting, and the guard escorted one of the women out. Another fight broke out and everyone, including Sandy, started running down the stairs to the exit.

I followed the crowd, hoping not to fall while running down three flights of stairs. Once I got outside I heard screaming and someone yelled,

"That bitch hit me in the face!" I flagged a cab and went home to write up my fieldnotes. I later learned that the fight broke out between two studs over a femme.[20] The sporadic violence along with the community and kinship relationships that Girlielicous provides many of Oakland's working-class queer Black women proves to be a complicated relationship affected by both external and internal forces of violence and societal marginalization, while offering a space for queer Black women to form community, and perform erotic shows for one another. Girlielicious offers employment for Black exotic dancers where their bodies are considered an asset; their erotic capital valued more than in male managed clubs. Also, the violence is among a few audience members, and not against dancers, making dancers feel safe performing at Girlielicious. The venue also serves as a way for Black queer performers to promote their show and generate business for themselves as exotic dancers by gaining regulars, performing at various Black lesbian events in Oakland, and using the Internet to promote their Web sites and upcoming shows.

5

Reproducing Cyber Desire

The Role of Technology and Desire Industries

Sometimes they use Mexican women who are made to look White, like
with blonde hair to advertise the club.

—Spice (reflecting on advertising techniques
in a San Francisco male-managed club).

Another way erotic capital is marketed within desire industries is through club
Web sites that advertise upcoming dancers, display images of club settings,
and show pictures of women, who really may not work there, to represent
the types of dancers employed at the club. Race is a central aspect in this
advertising of erotic capital because it is a signifier of dancer attractiveness
and desirability, and Web sites are geared toward a target audience based
on race, gender, class, and geographic setting. Advertising erotic capital via
the Internet is evident on the Web sites of Temptations, Conquest, and
Girlielicous.

The following content analysis of the Temptations Web site is from
2006 when the Web site had images of mostly White women, and 2007
when the club changed its marketing techniques, resulting in a new Web
site showing Black and Latina women, who are representative of the women
who worked there. However, although the second Web site is more diverse,
like the first one, it supports the valuing of symbolic White erotic capital,
and the marginalization of dark-skinned Black women.

On the 2006 Temptations home page, White and light-skinned Latina
women (with the exception of two light-skinned Black women) are used to
represent dancers at the club, activities, themes, and the type of customer
who patronize the club. The White women shown have blonde hair and
are thin, and the Latinas are olive- to fair-skinned with dark hair and slim
bodies. There are six photos featuring women: one blonde woman is dressed
as a dominatrix wearing leather and holding a whip. Below the words "After
Game Party," one woman with black hair, who could be Latina, sports a New

71

York Yankees logo on her hip, wearing a black- and white-striped thong, with a blue background, and the words "admit one" in red across her bare chest. Below the thong is the name of the club in red, white, and blue.

The photo positioned diagonally below it shows two Latina women (one brunette and one blonde) in two different positions. The brunette, who is facing the camera, wears a red top; the other photo is of her posing from a side view wearing a red bikini. The blonde is wearing a red leopard print top and red thong, and the other photo shows her topless with red dice surrounding her pelvic area. The background is red with the caption in gold letters reading: "Temptations Cabaret. Attention Dancers: Yankee Season is Back at Temptations. Make from $500 to $2,000 during game days . . . night and day shifts available. Call Today and Start Making Money Now." The photo next to it features a topless, olive-skinned Latina woman with dark hair. She is wearing a pink leopard print bottom and is standing against a pink leopard background. The words "Customer Appreciation Party" are printed next to her.

The photos indicate a certain working-class status of the club; the dice and gold letters give the advertisement a "bling"[1] effect. This effect can lower a dancer's erotic capital because the ad suggests a relaxed environment, offering more interaction with dancers, and resulting in a degraded club status, and a lack of standards regarding touching of the dancers.

Another photo features two women who could be White and/or Latina. They both have dark hair and are wearing black bikinis. They are positioned against a blue background containing pictures of women wrestling in erotic positions. The women also are in a pseudo-lesbian pose. The capture reads: "Oil wrestling Wednesday is back: Jump in the ring and wrestle with a beautiful Temptations girl. Wednesday May 17th." A last photo advertising a link for party services features three flashing pictures of women who appear to be either White or light-skinned Latinas.[2] One photo is of a blonde woman wearing a nightgown with stars covering her breast. She is holding a glass of champagne; the second flashing photo is of three White women kissing and undressing each other, and the third is of two White women who are topless. They are standing side-by-side; one wearing a pink skirt and heels, the other an open white vest and white bottoms.

These are the photos used to advertise the events at Temptations, the type of women who work there, and the experiences one can have there. The use of lesbianism also is a prominent theme of the Web site, which reflects the performance of sexuality of the lesbian and bisexual women who do work there. Lesbians who work as strippers often perform notions of heterosexuality to attract male clients; the nature of the job requires that women appear interested in the male customers. However, when lesbianism is present at a club it is performed and/or seen as being for the entertainment of the male customers and not for the dancer's own desire nor for the women who come as customers.[3] Not only can single women perform sexually for men, but men also can view two or more women performing for their benefit.

Symbolic Violence in the Advertising of Erotic Capital

The invisibility of Black women's bodies can contribute to a devaluing of their erotic labor in desire industries versus White women (and also some mixed-raced women of color) and actually encourage violence inflicted on them by customers, including a general neglect for their safety from bouncers and club owners.

In the category of club dancers at Temptations, the images shown are of platinum blonde White women (one looks like she could be a Latina). "Destiny" is wearing a pink sheer top and her hair is blowing in the wind. "Monet" is wearing a pink-flowered top; she has platinum blonde, shoulder-length hair. "Channel" is shown in front of a purple background. She is wearing a purple bikini and her raised arms reveal a slim waistline. "Madison" is wearing a black beret, gold necklace, and a lace teddy that outlines her breasts, which look like they might be implants.[4] The statement above the photos reads:

> To all the ladies, we have spared no expense in providing you with the state-of-the-art amenities. Featuring the largest dressing room in the state of New York, private showers and bathrooms, tanning beds and work-out facilities on the premises. Temptations is the finest club around. It is best known for having a variety of exotic women from all parts of the country and the world. Whatever your pleasure, blondes, brunettes, or redheads, the club features 50 to 100 ladies every evening.

This statement is interesting considering that the photos chosen do not reflect "exotic women from all parts of the country and the world." In the employment category are black-and-white photos of a blonde woman wearing a black-and-white polka-dot bikini. Above it a caption reads:

> If you're thinking about joining our team or becoming a Temptations Dancer, just send us an e-mail with a picture of a face shot, and a full body shot front and back, or call to make an appointment to come down for an interview.

To advertise bachelor parties given at Temptations, a black-and-white photo is used showing three White women (two brunettes and a blonde;

two are dressed in black teddies with white lace and thongs, the other is wearing a black bikini) massaging a topless, White, dark-haired male. The heading reads:

Looking for the ultimate Bachelor party headquarters?

At the Private Dining Room at Temptations you will find a service that cannot be matched in any other club in the nation, a high end dining room with the finest Gourmet Cuisine unmatched in the area. Have the finest of women presenting you food, drinks and champaigne all served with a warm smile. They are there to attend to your needs. There are Party packages to choose so please e-mail us to see if we fit your needs. **Send us an e-mail for party information and availability.**[5]

What is worth noting about this photo is that it shows not only the types of women who work there, but the kinds of men who are customers: white, fit, and middle class. This image is in direct contrast to the predominantly working-class men of color who attend the club and outnumber the few White men who patronize it in the afternoons and early evenings. It also represents a contradiction of aesthetics regarding why men go to Temptations, which usually is to get away from the mainstream blonde image of beauty, and because they like Black and Latina women with curves. The ads also illustrate a desired heterosexuality associated with class and race because the women are displayed as White and the only male in the ad is White.

Therefore, the Web sites are designed so that symbolically White, middle-class people can reproduce themselves as opposed to working-class people of color; even though this is the population that occupies Temptations as workers and customers. However, this marketing technique, like the emphasis on the club being on Park Avenue, may be a way to attract White businessmen who otherwise may not come to the Bronx, and increase their business clientele, while discouraging the younger, rowdier crowd.

The construction of whiteness is evident in the advertising of the Web site—all of the women are light-skinned Latinas or White non-Latina women; no Black women are featured on the Web site. Although it is true that many of the women who work at Temptations as dancers are Latina, not all are light-skinned with blonde hair; many are olive-toned with dark hair, and some Latinas would be classified racially as Black. The emphasis on whiteness regarding the women on the Web site is in sharp contrast to the neighborhood where Temptations is located, which has lots of Blacks and dark-skinned Latino/as.

This whitening of images of Latina/as is similar to what Twine (1997) found in her research on White supremacy in Brazil, where she analyzed the concept of *embranquecimento* (whitening). When discussing the White ideal of desire among Brazilians, Twine cited the media, mainly television, as being the one communicator of those ideals:

> The mass media in Brazil, particularly television, reflects and rein-forces the practice of embranquecimento by idealizing Brazilians who possess blonde hair, light-colored eyes, and other markers of European ancestry . . . this ideal is promoted both through both the predominance of blonde Euro-Brazilians in the mass media and the negative images of Afro-Brazilians and dark-skinned Brazilians. (pp. 89–90)

Temptations' Web site does not show negative images of Blacks, but in the absence of showing Black women (Latina and non-Latina) is the normal-ization of a White beauty aesthetic, which reinforces a form of aesthetic symbolic violence.

The normalization of whiteness in the representation of the Latinas featured on the site not only advertises the club's identity regarding the women who work there (most being from the Dominican Republic), but also the racial representations of who and what a Latina looks like. The association with a White ideal also merges with other associations of identity at Temptations, like the Yankees baseball team, which is viewed as a huge part of New York's identity as a city, but particularity part of the identity of the Bronx. Because baseball is viewed as an all-American sport, the intersections of whiteness, masculinity, and sports connect with consumptions of racialized desire—to be White (or White-looking) is seen as being all-American. The images used on the Temptations' Web site also contribute to the bodies of dark-skinned Black and Latina women having their erotic capital devalued (economically and physically), because the photos represent what is considered racially attractive and sexually desirable.

Temptations Diversified

The recent Temptations Web site shows Black and Latina women as dancers, which is reflective of the racial population that works there. Yet, the idea of whiteness and the overvaluing of Latinas with European ancestry is appar-ent on the Web site. Seventeen pictures appear on the Web site. There are seven Black women: one dark-skinned, with the other six being olive- to light-skinned and having straight hair. Of the other six Black women, all are thin except two who have curvy bodies, are light-skinned, and have short, dark, straight hair. The dark-skinned Black woman appears on the club's home page along with a light-skinned Latina woman with light brown hair; both the women are wearing bikinis—the Latina woman in a silver and pink bikini and the Black woman in a pink one. They have their backs to each other and the Latina woman is running her fingers through her hair while she looks at the camera. The Black woman is looking over her shoulder, her back facing the camera, and her bikini bottom pulled down, revealing her gluteal fold.

This photo of the Black woman reinforces the idea that the bodies of dark-skinned Black women are more sexually accessible than those of lighter skin and/or other races. The Latina woman in the photo is shown as being sexually desirable, with subjectivity compared with the Black woman, who only can be seen as a sexual object by revealing parts of her body considered, and normally clothed, for free. This image of the Black woman supports the feeling by some customers that they don't have to pay Black women the price they request for erotic services, such as lap dancing. This view contributes to the low erotic value of these women's bodies—the men believe they should get the Black women's services at a lower price, or for free.

The rest of the page shows an Asian woman (which the club has few of) positioned under the caption "Free Admission," which refers to a mailing list customers can sign up for to win a free admission pass. Another Latina woman, with very light skin, is seen representing the club's "MySpace" site.

The following seven images of Black women (all who look to be in their early 20s) are shown in portrait frames, which display them in various outfits and poses: a very light-skinned Black woman, who may be Latina, with short, straight, brownish hair, wearing gold heels, a white bracelet, a white bikini, and angel wings is shown sitting on a couch. A brown-skinned, curvy Black woman with short dark hair, is posed in a squatting position. She has a tattoo on her back and is wearing a pink teddy, pumps, and bunny ears resembling the Playboy image. Another light-skinned Black woman with long, black, wavy hair is standing up with her hand on her hip and wearing a white angel outfit. A light-skinned Black woman with medium dark straight hair is wearing a yellow-flowered bikini and is standing with her finger in her mouth. A light-skinned Black woman with long wavy hair poses in front of a car. She is wearing a black tank top with the club's name on it and a black thong. She is pouring water from a bottle over herself. (In two other photos, she is in the shower wearing a blue bikini, and her hair looks as though it has just been styled with a curling iron. A curvy light-skinned Black woman with short, dark, straight hair is pictured with her knees bent and wearing a black dominatrix outfit and holding onto a chain. The last photo shows a brown-skinned Black woman with curly brownish blonde hair with red highlights. She is wearing a black blazer, a black mini skirt, and no top. She is adorned with white pearls and is holding a ruler to cover her nipples, as she sits on a bar table—a sign advertising mixed drinks hangs next to her on the wall.

The Latinas represented in six images are light to olive complexion, and also look to be in their early 20s. The first image shows a Latina woman sitting against a mirror. She has an olive complexion and dark hair. She is pictured topless and has a white-trimmed mink draped over her shoulders just covering her breast. She is wearing a gold thong and matching heels. Another photo is of a light-skinned, voluptuous woman with light-brown ringlets. Her side is turned toward the camera and she is wearing a green hat and has a cigar in her mouth. Another photo is of a light-skinned woman kneeling on a couch with her back toward the camera. She is wearing a red thong, white knee-high stockings, black heels, red gloves, and a Santa Claus cap. She has a tattoo of a butterfly in the middle of her back. The next photo is a Saint Patrick's day-themed portrait of a woman sitting at a bar with a green tint in the background. She is wearing green pasties in the shape of four-leaf clovers, green and white knee-high stockings, a black hat, a green halter and white panties. She is holding a bottle of Jameson's Irish Whisky. The next photo was taken in a locker room, and shows a light-skinned Latina with blonde hair that shows her black roots. She is posing in black heels, Adidas knee socks, tight white shorts, and a white-striped vest, and is holding a baseball bat. one of the lockers is open, revealing a baseball bat with the Yankees logo. The last photo is of a light-skinned Latina with brown hair. She is on stage and is holding on to a pole. She is kneeling down with one knee bent and is wearing a red thong, a red halter, and sliver heels.

These newer photos definitely are more diverse and representative of the women who work at Temptations, and yet they reinforce the value of whiteness in the form of light skin and women who have physical features resembling European ancestry. The only dark-skinned Black woman is shown in a more revealing manner than her lighter-skinned peers, underscoring her lower erotic value.

Conquest on the Web

Conquest's Web site also advertises whiteness (with some exceptions) as a representation of the dancers who work there, and the experiences to be had there.[6] The club's home page has a red background featuring a head-shot of a woman, who looks White but could be Latina. She is wearing a red-and-white-striped bikini top with her hair up in pigtails. The other photo is of a blonde, White woman looking off to the side. She is dressed in a black bikini top and is standing under the sign for current events. The current events page has three photos of White women who are advertising different events.

The first photo is for private bachelor parties. The parties range from $170 per person for platinum packages, which include a four-course dinner, admission and 3 hours open bar, tax, and tip; $130 per person for the open bar packages, which include admission, 3 hours open bar, tax, and tip; and $110 per person packages that include admission, 2 hours open bar, tax, and tip. There also is the gold package, which cost $145 per person, and includes a four-course dinner, admission, and 2 hours open bar, tax, and tip. A White Latina woman wearing a black dress is shown smiling into the camera (a few months later this image was replaced by an Asian woman wearing heavy make up and a black-and-white bikini). The ad for upcoming happy hours for the clubs on the East and West side in New York features two blonde, White women (one wearing a black dress, the other dressed in hot pink) in a pseudo-lesbian pose.

The photo for the Conquest mall site shows a White woman with platinum blonde hair and pink lipstick. The mall site has White women modeling on the Conquest calendar. When the viewer clicks on the site a caption reads: "Warm Up With Gifts for Him or Her." A photo of two women appears in the middle of the screen: a blonde-haired White woman wearing a black blouse that reveals her cleavage, and a Black woman wearing a black straight wig styled in pigtails, red lipstick, and a black mole painted above her left lip. Even though the Black woman is dark-skinned, her look is Westernized by the style of her hair and the heavy make-up she wears.

Conquest also has club money called "Diamond Dollars." The photo advertising the club money shows a seductive White woman also with platinum blonde hair and wearing pink. The caption reads, "Tipping is Made Easy at Conquest with Diamond Dollars."

The club gallery and image page features photos of 10 women with the caption, "Conquest Dream Girls" placed above. The front photo, which is used to advertise this part of the Web site, features two White blonde-haired women holding each other in a playful pose. They are wearing Conquest attire: a baseball cap, tank top, and spandex shorts. The adjacent photos show three women who look to be Latina or of mixed race, five White women, and two White women holding each other in a pseudo-seductive pose. Another section of the Web site is the "wallpaper" site, which shows photos that customers can buy of three women (blondes and brunettes who look to be of mixed-race ancestry) in various poses.

The Web site does not show the Black and darker-skinned Latina women and men who work at the club as bouncers and janitors. This racial omission distorts the number of women of color who work at Conquest because they are not dancers or waitresses, and masks the racialized hierarchy of hiring practices at the club.

Similar to Temptations, Conquest uses images of mixed-race women (and White women) to advertise the identity of the club regarding potential dancers and customers. These images relate to taste, race, and class. However, unlike Temptations, Conquest is actually a well-known gentlemen's club with locations nationally; one can argue that the White middle-class–looking models reinforce the actual clientele of Conquest and the high status of the club, and not just how the club wishes to be seen.[7] The use of these women also underscores notions of a desirable heterosexuality pertaining to race and class. Although pictures of potential customers are not shown on Conquest's Web site as they are on Temptations' site, these notions still are communicated via the displaying of corporate earnings, suggesting a middle-class, possibly White male. This also is reinforced by the fact that whenever I conducted fieldwork at Conquest, there were few men of color in the audience, and if they were present, they were usually with White men.

The use of light-skinned models of color and/or White models to advertise Conquest buttresses the idea of this archetype of beauty as symbolic capital/profit and is viewed as a sure way to market the club. The notion of racial passing regarding whiteness also is prevalent on the Internet concerning how race is used in advertising fantasies online (Kolko, Nakamura, & Rodmann, 2000).

The concept of racial passing is noteworthy considering an individual can mask his or her true racial identity via the Internet. Clubs such as Temptations (on the first Web site) can disguise the identities of dancers and customers by posting images of White and mixed-race women as a kind of passing in their marketing, especially to customers who might not otherwise go to the Bronx. In the case of Conquest, racial passing in advertising is viewed as masking internal stratification of jobs, where most of the people of color work as bartenders, waitresses, masseuses, hostesses, and janitors.

One difference between marketing of Temptations and Conquest is the references to women on the sites. At Temptations there are theme nights advertised on the Web and emphasis is on the women who work there, or a constructed image of the women who worked there. However, the Conquest Web site is focused on club merchandise rather than on the women who work there—customers are visually experiencing the club more than the women. So, the erotic capital of the women who work at Conquest is competing against (and part of) the merchandise and status of the club. In fact, the only time women are the main focus of the site is on a MySpace[8] page created by the club as a self-promotion.[9] The MySpace page focuses on promoting images of women who work at Conquest by displaying a profile picture of a White male customer sitting between two White women—the caption reads: "The Most Beautiful Women in the World are Here at Conquest." The user of this site is profiled as a 27-year-old woman from New York, which is supposed to represent the age group of dancers at the club. The site's background colors are orange and yellow and shows photos of three blonde women: two looking away from the camera, and one wearing a red dress with her back to the camera. The other photos on the site feature White women with blonde hair (and a few brunettes) wearing lingerie and bikinis. One brunette is shown in black lingerie putting on stockings and a statement below reading:

We are also looking for models for our next promotional photo shoots, e-mail us if you are interested, please send a picture. Photo shoots are held in Manhattan in a professional studio.

Some other photos reveal women posing in a group with their backs to the camera. They are wearing T-shirts and tight Conquest shorts that highlight their butts—all are brunettes except for one blonde, and all looked tanned. In the middle of the page is a drawing of an Asian woman dressed in white lingerie. She has a leather strap across her shoulder, is wearing black gloves, with a sword on her back, and fire in the background. This photo makes her look like a powerful superhero, but also like the leather strap has her tied up: a cross between being dominant and submissive. Because this site is marketed toward (mostly White) men, the image can be read as supporting stereotypes of Asian women as submissive and needing to be controlled or as dragon ladies and conniving mistresses of White men.[10]

Further down the site is a section revealing 2,183 people listed as friends (although when I counted the photos on the site I counted only 906); categorized by race, I counted 188 White women, 500 White men, 24 Black women, 131 Black men, 24 Latinas, 15 Latinos, 13 Asian women, and 11 Asian men. These numbers are interesting considering that Black men represent a small number of actual customers and workers at Conquest; whereas the remaining figures closely represent the demographics of workers and customers based on race. The erotic capital of people of color (especially Black men) at Conquest is represented more via the Internet where they can be consumed rather than at the club, where bodies of color could directly benefit monetarily from this desire, especially as employees.

Conquest's MySpace page also communicates notions of liberal democratic pluralism and racial diversity through inclusion of people of color on the site and rap music on the profiles of some of the users, whereas the overall Web site is filled with White images of female beauty.[11] The racial representation of bodies on the Conquest MySpace page supports parallel narratives about beauty, race, virtual erotic capital, and desire.

Black Female Bodies:
Race, Community, and Lesbian Desire on the Internet

Silky also has a MySpace page under the category Silky Events. Unlike the Conquest and Temptations Web sites, which cater to middle-class White men and/or working-class men of color, the site for Girlielicous caters to Black lesbians. The advertisement features Silky sitting on a chair in the middle of four dancers, including Spice, Sandy, and two other dancers (all dark-skinned except for Spice). Silky is wearing grey slacks, a black jacket, white shirt, and a grey and pink tie, with a leg over one knee. The four dancers are surrounding her: Two dancers have their backsides facing the camera, and two are standing behind Silky. The ways these dancers market their erotic capital is evident in their outfits and shoes/boots: One dancer whose backside is facing the camera is wearing a turquoise bikini, matching garter belt, and clear stilettos. The dancer opposite her is wearing hot pink boots, fluorescent green fishnet stockings, gloves, and a thong with a white bikini top revealing a tattoo on her right arm. Spice is wearing a baby blue one-piece bathing suit, her blonde, curly locks neatly in place. The last dancer is wearing a hot pink top with long matching gloves; her hair is long, black, and wavy. The background of the flyer is black with fluorescent pink captions reading:

> **Women Loving Women Event**
> **Silky Presents**
> **Xtreme Show**
> **Every Second and Third Saturday of the Month**
> **$8 before 10:30, $10 after**

Also, in the background is a rainbow flag representing queer community and identity. It is obvious from the flyer that this is a Black lesbian event emphasizing forms of erotic capital, such as the rear end and curvy bodies, that are considered desirable and create value for Black beauty standards. The Web site for Silky Productions provides this alternative space to value Black erotic capital from a queer and working-class perspective. Silky also has a personal page on MySpace that shows her dressed in a white suit, gold chain, and holding a cane; she is shown with her wife, also a Black woman dressed in a white fur coat opened to reveal a black halter and a tattoo near her heart. A photo next to it shows Silky actually performing, which is rare. She is wearing her usually curly hair straight, a sequined gold skirt, false eyelashes, gold heels, and a black blouse. The photos show her dancing on stage for Black and Latina women.

The page displays Silky's ability to perform masculine and feminine types of gender presentation and the desirable erotic capital for each: pimp attire for her masculine persona, and form-fitting sequined dresses and make-up for her feminine attire. Silky refutes the racialized stereotype of the "stone butch" of color (Halberstam, 1998) not identifying with femininity because she is able to perform her "feminine" side, while identifying as a stud.

However, although Silky is able to get out of stereotypes associated with being a stud, or a butch, relating to gender performance on her site, her persona as a pimp (the white suits, cane, and gold chains) still associates Black masculinity with the controlling image of being a pimp, even though it may be a parody on this stereotype as was implied in my interview with Silky in the previous chapter. The remaining photos on Silky's site show various dancers who performed at the club for a Valentine's Day event. Sandy is shown wearing a black-and-white-striped half jacket with a hood and pink trimmings, matching leggings, a pink thong, and white heels. She is dancing with a heavy-set Black woman with short, straightened brown hair. Sandy almost resembles Grace Jones with her androgynous look; her hair is straight and black and she is wearing copper-colored eye shadow. In other photos she is viewed wearing a hot pink bikini and matching earrings, highlighting her dark skin, and dancing with a Black stud who is wearing a white baseball cap, blue sweat paints, and blue sports jacket.

One dancer is an overweight Black woman, with a brown complexion. She is wearing a rainbow-print dress showing bruises on her knees—an example of alterative forms of erotic capital valued in this Black women's space that probably would not have a positive exchange value in clubs like Conquest or Temptations (although Temptations has more flexibility in categories of beauty than Conquest). Another dancer who goes by the name "Miss Money" is bald. She is wearing glasses, a sheer black teddy, black boots, orange earrings, and has a tattoo of a rose on her thigh. The photos show women giving her money for her performance. Other site photos are of Spice on stage wearing a red dress, a white boa, and blue eye shadow. She is shown from various positions: front, side, and back, revealing a curvy figure.

In another photo, a dark-skinned Black woman is featured giving lap dances. She is wearing a pink-, green-, and yellow-striped bikini top, a pink bikini bottom, neon green fishnets, and has curly black hair extensions. Another photo is of a dark-skinned woman wearing a pink-and-blue bikini with a sheer blue top and white-and-blue bikini bottom; her hair is long brown and looks to be a weave. She has tattoos above her breast, arms, and thighs. The last photo is of a dancer named Sassy, who is light-skinned with short, straight spiked dark hair and a thin but muscular body. She is shown in a hot pink bikini with a black skull on the left side. She has tattoos on her shoulder and breast and exudes a tough femme persona that again offers alternative forms of erotic capital to be valued for and among Black women.

The remaining photos of the site are of Silky and her son, and the dancers performing on various nights at a venue called the Lavender Room (including one butch woman rapper performing with men, and one Asian woman who is sitting in the background with a cast on her leg, but also performing with them) emphasizing erotic capital such as curves, rear ends, with focus on gender performance, and creativity in costume design. Flyers of dancers also are shown on the site, illustrating diversity in dancer bodies, language,[12] and skin tones. Unlike the ads for Conquest and Temptations, the photos reflect real diverse images of the women who work there. They also convey a sense of community among the women as they are performing for different events at the space, which frequently includes photos of Silky receiving lap dances at the events she hosts. In addition to Silky's site, individual dancers also have sites.

Blogs,[13] Community, and Erotic Capital

Spice's Web site consists of a rosy red background and a blurb advertising her services as an exotic dancer. The blurb includes a PayPal account. There are pictures of her wearing boas, bikinis, boots, and thongs while performing at club events for women. Some of the photos show her bottomless. In other photos she is on a red couch and is wearing a pink dress, white pearls, and gold shoes; her hair is styled to resemble a model from the 1950s. Spice's erotic capital is the subject of the site, her form of expressing subjectivity, autonomy, and providing sexual images for Black lesbians, which is making Black queer women visible, desirable subjects in their own right.

Other than selling her erotic capital and services, Spice's site also connotes a notion of community among the women dancers, promoters, and audience. The photos chosen to appear on her site promote female unity, love, and camaraderie. One photo shows a baby chick and a gray kitten with a caption that reads: Blonde Chick with Nice Pussy; another photo shows a cartoon image of a young brown woman with baggy jeans, halter, and long hair and the captions reads: "Jealously is a Terrible Disease. Get Well Soon." Personal photos in the "friends" section of her page show Spice with her girlfriend, butch queer Latina/Filipina rapper JenRo, gay Black male friends, Black and Latina women friends, and other fellow dancers of color. The names of the dancers of color are racialized such as Black Magic, Thickness, and Cinnamon.

In the "blog" section of Spice's MySpace page are entries pertaining to various issues in her life, such as returning to school for her undergraduate degree, promotions of future shows, the murder of a Black male friend, and advice on how new dancers should negotiate money and perform at shows. Regarding the murder of a young Black friend, she writes:

> I don't know if anybody my age will make it to "Die of natural causes." I damn sure wish that young black men would stop killing each other, but that is easier said than done.

After her posting, a few MySpace friends offer their support and comment on the internalized forces of racism that creates intra-violence in Black and Latino/communities. Although there is commentary on violence among Black men in East's Bay Black community, there is no comment on lesbian violence. However, the commentary illustrates the ways erotic capital intersects with larger structural issues, such as urban violence and poverty.[14]

The second blog on Spice's MySpace page addresses the issues of dancers and money. The title of the blog is called, "Stripper Game Should Not be the Ripper Game," and encourages dancers, especially new ones, to not give their services away for free. For example, regarding private parties, Spice advises dancer to charge for performances and to check with her regarding standard prices for dances. She makes the distinction between "performance" and "freak show" when referring to dancers who, hoping to make extra money, insert unclean objects into their vaginas during a public show. In actuality, these actions hurt their cash flow because the dancers should be performing these acts as and charging the price of a private show.[15]

Spice points out that explicit performances not only undercut dancers, but they also hurt the venues because liquor and nudity on stage is illegal. These venues (which are few and far between for Black lesbians in Oakland) can lose their liquor license or be fined if they are raided. This aspect of Spice's blog speaks to the connection among sexuality, race, and class when operating erotic establishments. Although clubs that are located in poor/working-class communities of color are raided by police for drugs and prostitution, clubs in wealthier and White areas are not subject to raids and police harassment. Black lesbian clubs in Oakland often are unfairly targeted for raids because of their position within urban space, sexuality, class, and race. Thus, Spice's blog is a call to maintain the space Black queer women have available to them in the East Bay, have dancers be paid what they are worth, and continue to promote erotic autonomy and visibility among queer Black women.

Both Girlielicious and the current Temptations Web sites provide Black and Latina women with erotic representation otherwise not found on mainstream Web sites, such as the one owned by Conquest. However, on the current Temptations Web site, women of color, with the exception of one Black woman, are marketed in ways that resemble White beauty standards (light skin, long straight hair); whereas the Girlielicious Web site (along with individual dancer sites) offers the most diversity for marketing the erotic capital of Black women, showing their bodies as full-figured, and in various skin tones. The Girlielicious site reinforces the multiple functions of women performing erotic entertainment for each other (community-building, sexual entertainment, employment), by dancers marketing their erotic capital, sharing advice on how to make money, and advertising various weekly events in order to attract the Black queer women of the East Bay.

6

Labor Stratification in Desire Industries

Colorism, Citizenship, and Erotic Capital

During the day you usually find Asian and Latina dancers, a few Black
dancers, and most are thin. Also, when you work during the day the stage
fee is lower, it's $60 as opposed to $100. At night you get a rowdier crowd,
so Black women have to put up with that more, because that's when most
of us are scheduled.

—Sonya (23-year-old Black dancer at Temptations)

Dancers at both Temptations and Conquest are stratified along the basis
of skin color, language accent, and body type. Dancers with lighter skin
tones generate the highest erotic capital from customers.[1] Sociologists have
documented the historical legacy of lighter-skinned Black women holding a
higher market and sexual value compared with darker-skinned Black women.
In *Race, Ethnicity, and Nation* Joane Nagel (2003) affirms that during slavery,
lighter-skinned slaves were worth a higher price within the slave market and
were more sexually desired by White male slave owners:

> Another incentive for white men to have sex with black women
> was the monetary and symbolic worth of their mixed-race or
> "mulatto" offspring. Lighter-skinned slaves fetched a higher price
> at market and occupied a higher status in the cultural system of
> slaveowning society: they were more likely to be employed in
> slaveowners' homes rather than in their fields and more likely to
> be the objects of their male masters' lust. (p. 107)

Similarly, Patricia Hill Collins (1990) notes the current divisions between
lighter- and darker-skinned Black women and the advantage light-skinned
Black women have within White-dominated institutions:

> Institutions controlled by Whites clearly show a preference
> for lighter-skinned Blacks, discriminating against darker ones

or against any African-Americans who appear to reject White
images of beauty. (p. 91)

I found lighter-skinned Black and Latina dancers were preferred by
customers patronizing the desire industries I researched. I also found that
internal stratification occurred among workers at the same club concerning
race and occupation, which reflected internal stratification based on race in
other occupations (Bourgois, 2003; Waldinger, 1996; Williams, 2006). In
clubs such as Conquest, which are predominately White, people of color
(especially immigrants) are employed in lower-tier positions (e.g., coat check
workers, bathroom attendants, bouncers), whereas White women are employed
as dancers, the main attraction for the venue. In clubs like Temptations in
which dancers are mainly people of color, dancers are scheduled for desirable
and undesirable shifts based on race and body type. Both types of stratification are documented in fieldnotes discussed here.

Racial Stratification at Conquest

During one of my field observations at Conquest, I decided only to observe
dancer and customer interactions rather than interview anyone. This decision
came after the manager expressed that he did not like me taking notes and
chatting with customers the last time I was there. I apologized, paid my $30
entrance fee, and told him that I would just observe. It was 9 p.m. on a
Saturday, and the club only had been opened an hour. I checked my bag at
the coat check where a Latina was working behind the desk and then took
a seat. The club was almost empty; I sat toward the back near the bar. I was
one of four customers; the others were a White male–female couple, and a
White man to the far right. Again, I was the only woman there alone, and
on that night, the only Black customer.

A White dancer was performing for the couple. She was thin and
looked as if she may have had breast implants; she danced to Stevie B's
"Dreaming of Love." The DJ was a White man with thick dreadlocks. He
had a deep, penetrating voice. He introduced each dancer and informed the
audience who would be coming on stage next. I looked up at the TV screens;
there were six all together (three in the front, three in the back). The screens
in the front showed an ad for Conquest with two White women swinging
on poles, a boxing match, and commercials for various products. The three
screens in the back showed the same things as the screens in the front. A
couple of waiters walked back and fourth making sure customers had drinks.
The entrance to the restaurant was next to the stage.

As I watched the dancers perform their 15-minute sets to three songs,
I noticed something that I didn't notice the first time I was at the club:

Almost all the dancers were White, but the bartenders, bouncers, waiters, janitors, and masseuses were ethnically diverse, including White (Russian), Latina, Indian, Asian, and Black.

During my 4-hour stay, I observed that out of 16 dancers who performed, one was Black and one looked to be bi-racial (White and Asian descent), as opposed to three of four masseuses being women of color (one Asian, one dark-skinned Latina, one Indigenous looking Latina with an olive complexion). Of the four bouncers, one was Black, the other three men looked Italian, or of eastern European descent. Of the three women greeting customers and checking in their coats, two were Latina; and three of the four bartenders were Latina. I then began to notice the different ways erotic capital was marketed, stratified, and sold within these various groups of employees.

Women who worked as masseuses and bartenders had less opportunity to market their erotic capital compared with dancers, but unlike bartenders, they at least had the chance to walk up to customers and ask them if they wanted a massage, thus displaying themselves to customers. During my stay, I noticed that of the four masseuses, the two Latinas did not sell any $20 massages to customers. I observed two White men, one of who bought a massage from a White dancer, whereas the other man didn't seem to spend much money. The darker-skinned Latina sat at the table and asked him if he wanted to buy a massage from her, he smiled, and politely told her no. Throughout the evening, she returned to the table to talk, however, despite her attempts she never sold him a massage. A few other White dancers also visited this table, but the customer declined to spend any money on lap dances or massages. Although the Latina masseuse continued asking other White customers if they wanted massages, none seemed interested in buying one from her.[2]

When I asked Cristina about situations like the one just described, she replied that White customers viewed women of color as having less erotic value than White women:

> I think White guys really like women of color because they think we are exotic, like a trophy, because of our curves and color. They like what is on the outside, but not on the inside. I feel like they don't want to know the inside, we are just a commodity to them.

Cristina's observation can be applied to interpersonal relationships between White men and women of color, and also to the marginalization of the economic advancement of women of color who are employed within desire industries (i.e., because women of color are viewed as more exotic, they are not the norm, so customers may feel more comfortable spending money on White women's erotic services).

Diana, who works at Conquest, is originally from New York City, and
although was living in Florida, she had come back to New York to make
some extra money. She is 19 and of German and Puerto Rican ancestry. She
is attending college to become a medical technician and is dancing as a way
to earn extra money. When I asked her how she felt being a Latina in the
exotic dance industry, she said that her race is an asset in making money in
the exotic dancing industry:

> Yes, because I'm Latina, I'm blonde . . . I could be a lot of
> things . . . people don't really know what I am. I can play on
> that . . . I can be whatever they want me to be.

Diane's responses say a lot about race and class. She feels her race is an
asset in dancing primarily because she is mixed, and can therefore "perform"
various races for customers. In other words, they can imagine her to be the
race of their choice, and even can ignore the fact that she is Latina, instead
seeing her as a White blonde. This example of racial "morphing" brings into
question who is able to perform whiteness, and the ways the category of
whiteness can expand to include groups previously not categorized as White
(Twine & Warren, 1997). For example, if Diana were part Black, would she
be able to pull off her racial performance? If so, what desired racial makeup
would she be?

Mona, a 26-year-old dancer who works at Temptations, could pass for
a dark-skinned Latina, but she is Italian, Irish, and Black. When I asked
her how she markets herself racially, she replied:

> At Temptations, it didn't matter since most women at the club
> are Latinas, but when I work in Manhattan, I never say I am
> Black because the customers don't like Black girls, I always say
> I am Italian and play up my Italian accent.

Skin color stratification was further underscored by Casey, a 22-year-old
light-skinned Black Puerto Rican dancer at Temptations. Casey said that
although the club hired Black and Latina women, dark-skinned Black women
usually were discouraged from working there:

> Often when dark-skinned Black women audition they are not
> hired the way light-skinned Latina and Black women are. Once
> around six dark-skinned Black women auditioned and none where
> hired. When I asked the management why, they said too many
> dark-skinned women would make the club lose money.

Skin color differences, as well as class differences, among dancers affects club image, especially regarding prostitution in clubs. Cristina, similar to Natasha, had worked as a waitress in a racially diverse working-class club in Queens, but stopped because she felt prostitution was occurring at the club:

> There were a lot of Black, Indian, and Latino customers there; overall they were okay. The Jewish guys also were nice, but the WASP guys were not nice. Also, the money was pretty bad at that time. You could be there 8 hours and only make $100. I sometimes made $2,500. There were all kinds of women: light-skinned Italian women, Black skinny, busty women. There were actually more White women at that time than women of color.

Cristina observed that the club's marketing image changed to reflect the influx of women of color hired at Conquest; however, she said that they were hired when the market was on a downturn, which equates women of color with low erotic value. Her analysis of this hiring process reflects other labor fields in which people of color are hired for a job during undesirable times (Waldinger, 1996). The stratification of women of color in the exotic dance industry parallels job queues and gender segregation of women's employment in traditionally "male" occupations—the value of these jobs decrease once women enter into them (Reskin, 1990).

Desire, Assimilation, and Citizenship

One of the ways citizenship is exercised in this country is via assimilation into U.S. society and culture, especially within areas of work. In desire industries, issues of race and job stratification complicate the route of assimilation for immigrants and U.S.-born people of color, based on factors, such as race and class. For U.S.-born Black women, Latinas, and immigrant workers of color in desire industries, citizenship status is challenged by a process of exclusion and stratification that mirrors other labor markets. The notion of assimilation historically has applied to European immigrants on their entry into the United States during the mid-1800s. According to sociologist Robert Park (1950), immigrants in the United States adapted to life by contact, competition, accommodation, and finally assimilation. Although this process would be harder for first-generation European immigrants, it would be easier for the second generation and harder for Blacks and Asians who were seen as more racialized than European immigrants (Frazier, 1957; Kornblum, 1974; St. Clair & Cayton, 1945). In *Race and Culture*, Park (1950) argues that

European immigrant groups assimilate based on skin color, but Japanese immigrants had a cumbersome attempt at assimilation because of their skin color—this was especially true for Black people, along with Latinao/s. However, Parks contradicts his views on the physical barriers for people of color, especially Blacks, to successfully assimilate because of skin color differences, and uses situations with European immigrants (e.g., Jewish people) to argue that once discrimination was removed, assimilation would be possible. Many scholars have refuted the universal application of the European-based model of citizenship and assimilation, arguing that because of institutional racism, people of color were denied full citizenship rights, especially in areas of education, housing, government, law, industry, and media (Collins, 2000; Chang, 2002; Glenn, 2002; Jacobson, 1998; Romero, 2002).

Another vehicle through which people can gain citizenship and move toward assimilation is in the realm of beauty. Cultural sociologists have studied the connection between beauty and citizenship especially among women in two areas: plastic surgery and beauty pageants. Elizabeth Haiken (1997), in her book *Venus Envy: A History of Cosmetic Surgery*,[3] examines the role of cosmetic surgery in assimilation among eastern Europeans immigrating to the United States during the early 20th century. Haiken states:

> For those whose features fell short of this standard, cosmetic surgery offered hope. In general, prospective patients viewed surgery as an option according to the amount of prejudice they encountered, the identifiability as ethnic of particular features, the availability of surgical techniques to eradicate the offending features, and money. In the early decades of the twentieth century, Jews and Italians most often met these criteria. They were (or thought to be) identifiable to American eyes; they encountered prejudice; the feature that most troubled them was the nose, against which surgical techniques had already proved effective; and they were upwardly mobile. (p. 181)

During my research, I saw the connection between European beauty standards and upward mobility among immigrant workers at Conquest. I met a few dancers from Russia who, based on outer appearances, blended in with White U.S.-born dancers. I only knew they were from Russia either because of their accent or because they told me when I asked them how they began dancing. They usually responded by telling me they knew someone else who was dancing and that they had immigrated from Russia. Even though the Russian dancers I met did not, to my knowledge, have any plastic surgery,[4] the discourse concerning cosmetic surgery as a venue for assimilation among European immigrants is valid when examining different outcomes among immigrants who worked at Conquest and Temptations.

However, I also met many U.S. and non U.S.-born Blacks and Latino/as (along with men from India) who were janitors and/or bathroom attendants at Conquest, opposed to one Russian male who worked as a bouncer.

For example, Lilia is a 45-year-old bathroom attendant from the Dominican Republic. She also works at Home Depot. She has an olive complexion and speaks with an accent. She explained that she doesn't make good money at Conquest, and has to pay for supplies such as snacks, lotion, hand soap, hair spray, and other items for the dancers while they take their cigarette breaks in the bathroom. She has to pay $40 to work (and buy supplies) but hopes to make that back in tips. Unfortunely, she hardly does, so often she ends up not making any money al all.

Denise is a waitress at Conquest. She also is from the Dominican Republic and has a brown skin tone. When I asked about her job, she stated the following:

> I have worked at Conquest about 6 months. It's all right. My mother works here as a janitor, so that's how I got the job. I commute 2 hours from Staten Island.

Both of these women's answers illustrate that their path into working in the sex industry is through other service-sector jobs, which resembles the path of many immigrant women of color into the U.S. labor market.[5] Their responses also underscore the difference between White immigrants who can assimilate into the U.S. labor market and immigrants of color who cannot. For example, although the Russian dancers had accents that marked them as immigrants, they were able to blend in with other White dancers in marketing their erotic capital as dancers; however, the few light-skinned Latina dancers did not have accents but still could not blend in. The Latinas working outside the dancer category were darker-skinned, and some had accents, underscoring the degree to which they did not assimilate into the White structure of Conquest and, thus were economically and racially stratified into lower-tier positions.

This stratification process also affected male immigrants of color and their entry into the exotic dancer industry. Tommy describes his trajectory into becoming manger of Temptations:

> I was a used car dealer here in the Bronx. You know, I'ma tell you something right now, it's hard out here for a Black man to get a job . . . you do whatever you can get. I was a good car dealer and a good strip club owner.

Hassan, a 30-year-old immigrant from India worked at Dunkin' Donuts before taking a job as a male bathroom attendant at Conquest:

It's a job like any other, before this I worked at Dunkin' Donuts for minimum wage, this is not that different—I get tips here, I don't plan to do this forever.

Examples such as this point to what many sociologists say is the current struggle of the working poor to survive with low-paying jobs, as well as illustrating the fact that different racial groups are channeled into different jobs, making the immigrant experience different for various groups coming to the United States.

Discipline and Punishment at Temptations

Many women who work at Temptations complain about the lack of security available to dancers, especially during late night shifts. At the same time, dancers and owners are concerned about random raids by undercover police in order to make sure the club is obeying legal codes regarding the operating of strip clubs (i.e., no prostitution). The relationship between over- and underpolicing of Temptations, and by extension the South Bronx, resembles the control Michel Foucault (1975) spoke of in *Discipline and Punish: The Birth of the Prison* regarding the role of the prison and the development of discipline of docile bodies so that workers can perform duties for a new industrialized society. One method of control was through the creation of the panopticon to monitor the prisoner's body. This form of discipline and punishment does not have to occur in prisons. Heavy policing of people and communities, such as in many inner-city communities of color, also can be carried it out in similar fashion, such as through a strong police presence, which leads people to feel as though they are being watched. Yet with heavy policing comes the issue of underpolicing, which illustrates the devaluing of public safety of inner-city residents.[6]

This analysis of underpolicing and deviancy is useful to situate the lack of security at Temptations regarding the safety of the women of color who work there, as well as in other clubs. Natasha remembered times she felt unsafe working at a strip club in Manhattan. She said that although she felt unsafe, her boyfriend at the time would never pick her up, illustrating the devaluing of the safety of Black women in desire industries:

He wouldn't pick me up from FlashDancers if I were working late, like until 5 in the morning. He would call and see if I made it in but he never picked up me. When I asked him why, he said he felt I was safe with the cab; but other women had their boyfriends pick them up.

When I attended Temptations again to conduct fieldwork, I was accompanied by one of my White male friends. I went with him to Kentucky Fried Chicken, where he ordered a chicken sandwich and we passed a homeless-looking Black man outside of the restaurant. I observed the signs on the wall for a meal large enough to fit on a laptop, called the laptop meal, one encouraging customers to "go large" and order a "kitchen fresh" large-sized meal, and another for customers to enter a contest and win up to $1,000. I also noticed that customers had to order through bulletproof glass.[7]

We entered the club and because it is before 7 p.m. we were not charged a cover fee. I observed new artwork of Latina women dancing. There was also drilling and construction work going on, which I found odd to be happening during business hours. I watched the dancers perform on stage and noticed the customers sitting in the main area, mainly in groups of three or more. One group of customers consisted of three Black men and one Black woman, who was casually dressed in jeans and an orange sweatshirt. The men also were wearing orange and blue jeans. The woman was well integrated into the group and from my observation of her body language and demeanor, appeared to be a lesbian. From her masculine presentation, I perceived her as "one of the guys."

In the middle of my visit, I witnessed a young Black man approach the stage where a dark-skinned Black woman was performing. He tipped her by putting the money between her thighs and thong. In and of itself, this was not a problem because it is a popular form of tipping, however, the man proceeded to smack and rub the dancer's rear.

I noticed that Black customers who were reprimanded by the bouncers for rowdy behaviors were the customers who touched dark-skinned dancers the most and did not tip them. This reinforced the hypersexualization and low erotic capital of the dark-skinned dancers. One customer in particular, was behaving in an inappropriate manner and appeared to be drunk. He approached a Latina dancer who offered him a lap dance. Within 5 minutes of the performance, she stopped and walked away from him. He persisted by approaching other dancers on stage, as well as offering the waitresses money, without buying a drink. I could tell the women were uncomfortable by the way they smiled and told him, "No thanks," but he continued to invade their personal space. Meanwhile, although one of the bouncers was positioned near the stage, watching, he did not intervene.

I was concerned about the low-level of security this club offered, and cannot imagine a similar situation occurring at Conquest. In fact, during one of my visits to Conquest a middle-aged White man was yelling at the bouncer on duty and actually taking swings at him. He was escorted out of the club. Soon thereafter, I heard an ambulance siren and learned the man had been drunk and suffered a heart attack while swinging at the bouncer. The police did not have to come because the bouncer successfully took care of the situation—and the club's image was not tarnished because of the incident.

However, sometimes customers will attempt to protect dancers from potentially violent customers. Mike says that often he will stay late and escort dancers to the subway station or a cab:

> I often close the place out, so when the night shift ends at 4 a.m. I often walk dancers to the subway or hail a cab for them, but usually the customers are fine. It's leaving the club that's dangerous. The hood needs this, it's a place for men to hang out and release frustration . . . it's better than being on the street.

Mike's statement suggest that Temptations is a social space that actually brings a sense of social order to the neighborhood and a place where men can occupy themselves rather than being on the street and possibly engaging in antisocial behavior.

A few nights later, a male Puerto Rican friend and I stopped into Temptations to observe levels of exchanges between dancers and customers. A bouncer checked our ID, frisked us, and checked our bags before we entered, further highlighting the practice of policing in venues located in communities of color. He told me people have been known to carry guns into the club, which is why they have frisk customers and search their bags. This time I was able to obtain more interview material from dancers and customers. When I asked customers why they preferred Temptations to other clubs in the Bronx, they overwhelmingly expressed the fact that it was considered the classiest club in the Bronx, which often meant it was less violent. Jamal, a 28-year-old Black man stated:

> The other clubs are, well . . . ghetto. This is classy. You have stages; the women are pretty. The other places are just bars without real stages. I like to just come in here with a friend, drink, and chill. It's not as hood like the other ones, where the customers get real rowdy.

Sheila, a 23-year-old Black dancer, explained why she felt Temptations was different than other clubs in the Bronx, but cautioned against stating that Temptations didn't share any elements of seedy behavior with the other surrounding clubs:

> At Temptations the girls do audition, whereas at the other clubs often there is no audition, and you can almost just come in from off the street. So, in that case it has more class than other

clubs. But on the other hand, it is still ghetto . . . for example, after midnight the crowd goes from businessmen to younger, rowdier guys. So, you get some yelling, people are frisked for guns—although there are fewer fights here than at other clubs, but occasionally there are police raids.

Sonya, another Black dancer, who is 23-years-old, a graduate of Penn State, and works at Crunch Gym during the week, said she works at Temptations for extra money on weekends. Sonya felt there was a form of racial stratification among dancers, and that Black and heavier dancers were scheduled more on the night shift when the stage fee is higher, and customers are younger, rowdier, and mostly Black and Latino, rather than in the afternoon when customers tend to be older, racially mixed, and includes White businessmen:

> I feel it's hard for Black women to make money because you compete with the lighter-skinned women and thinner women. I am skinny, so I work in the daytime. I worked at night once, but stopped because I didn't feel safe.

Sonya's description of the internal racial stratification of Temptations differs from the stratification at Conquest, where most people of color work the floor, whereas most of the dancers are White and gain the maximum benefits of working there. In this case, it highlights divisions among women of color within the same status of being dancers. Non-Black Latinas, and mixed-raced women of color have higher erotic capital than dark-skinned Black women; as a result dancers are tipped more and work more desirable shifts (in this case a desirable shift means a less rowdy crowd, although the night shift is where more money can be made, but dancers also pay more of a stage fee).

These accounts of customer and dancer interactions are examples of the ways space inform desire. Ideas of status and group membership among friends, gender, and race inform how customers interact with dancers, and the exchanges that occur within these spaces.

Black and Latina women's notion of citizenship was challenged via a process of marginalization and exclusion at both clubs in the arena of desire and job status. Similar to jobs in the service industry, Latina/os often were employed as janitors and Black men as security at Conquest. This invisibility of people of color employed in these sectors at Conquest mirrors Anne McClintock's (1995) theory of creating empire within concepts of leisure and work that separated servants from housewives during the Victorian era.

The fact that both Conquest and Temptations are regarded as gentlemen's clubs, but separate regarding geographic settings, race, and class emphasizes the idea of "separate but equal" prior to integration policies of the Civil Rights Movement, mirroring similar institutions (schools, bathrooms, housing, water fountains, swimming pools) where faculties in Black and Latino spaces were inferior to ones in White spaces, and the races were separated by de jure institutionalized racism.

As the service sector expands, especially within the era of globalization, many workers will enter the sex industry (or other desire industries) to varying degrees. Therefore, it is important for feminist labor rights scholars to recognize all the ways that capital can be achieved and exchanged, erotic capital being one variable in how women (in this study Black and Latina women) move up or down job queues. Racial stratification regarding income attainment and educational advancement affects women, with lighter-skin women being able to accrue more of these resources. So, as feminist scholars fight for labor rights within the service industry, challenging and recognizing the ways erotic capital functions to stratify workers will be crucial toward achieving the goals of labor and immigrant rights for women.

7

Conclusion: Race Versus Taste

Symbolic Racism in the Post-Civil Rights Era

On March 7, 2007 I appeared on National Public Radio's (NPR) *News and Notes* on the Sex and Sexuality series hosted by Farai Chideya. I was asked to discuss my attempts to get more Black women hired at the Lusty Lady, as well as my research on the racial stratification of Black and Latina women in the exotic dance industry. I talked about the ways Black and Latina women are hypersexualized (meaning overly sexualized compared with White women) through media images, especially in music videos, which usually show women of color in skimpy clothing supporting male rapper subjectivity. I stated that because images of women of color in the sex industry are made so accessible through the media, male customers frequently underpay them for sexual services. A few days after NPR aired the show, a man from San Francisco wrote a letter in response to my comments stating that sex work is about fantasy, and one cannot impose fantasies on customers through affirmative action. He continued his letter by stating that Blacks are at the bottom of being viewed as desirable fantasy objects, and that the only way they will be viewed as more sexually desirable is if they improve the public image of their community and increase their wealth.

This man's comment speaks toward the public response I encountered while examining racial stratification among Black and Latina exotic dancers in the sex industry. Racism against Black women in this industry is usually viewed as normal because, like other appearance-based industries (such as modeling, acting), the sex industry is based on ideas of customer taste and preference. Thus, if Black women are not desirable, it is the objective result of customer taste within a free market—not structural anti-Black racism operating within the psyche of the customer or club management.

The letter also supports neo-liberalist ideas regarding the responsibility of Blacks to control their media image, and to improve their wealth status. Both of these views reinforce the belief that Black people are to blame for their negative public image, for having less wealth than Whites, and therefore having lower erotic capital value in the exotic dance industry.[12]

When it comes to issues of racial segregation and systemic discrimination in a post-Civil Rights era, many people, including some people of color, subscribe to the idea that racism does not exist in ways that hinder people of color from advancing economically, and that poor U.S.-born Blacks and Latino/as do not want to work hard. They believe that everyone has the same opportunities to advance within the current socioeconomic structure. This viewpoint is prevalent regarding Black women in the exotic dance industry, as evidenced by the letter responding to the NPR interview. What is missing from this position of the free-market and customer taste choice model is the role of structural and symbolic racism and classism within the exotic dance industry, as well as other industries.

My research shows that contrary to the notion that male customer taste is objective, it is carefully socially constructed through club marketing techniques, as well as the media at large, which overproduces images of White and mixed-race people as sexually desirable. There are more images of Black people in the media (and now of Latino/as) especially in films, which challenge stereotypes of Blacks being lazy, hypersexualized, and/or violent. However, images with these messages targeting Black women constantly are reinforced in other forms of media, such as gangsta rap videos, which give men of all races distorted and racist sexist ideas about Black and Latina women. The news is another form of media that supports ideas about Black and Latina women by focusing on them as welfare recipients in need of former President Bill Clinton's 1996 welfare reform policy, or as undocumented immigrants, taking advantage of hard-working tax paying citizens. As demonstrated in my findings, these images of Black and Latina women have consequences that affect the life chances of Black and Latina women in the exotic dance industry by influencing how they are positioned and treated regarding skin color stratification, job rank, safety, and earnings.

Spaces that provide sexual entertainment in Oakland for lesbian and queer-identified working-class Black women also are tied into larger urban structures. However, for queer Black women, the marketing of erotic capital is a way to form community and exercise autonomy, not just an avenue for making money as exotic dancers. Additionally, these spaces both challenge and reinforce notions of patriarchy and masculinity, while responding to the specific needs and desires of working-class Black lesbians who mostly are ignored by mainstream White-dominated gay and lesbian institutions.

In a post-Civil Rights era in which a Black and Latino/a consumer-based middle class has increased,[2] (although still a minority compared with the White middle class), there are more media representations geared toward these groups (i.e., *Essence* and *Latina* magazines, which illustrate Black and light-skinned Latina women in respectable heterosexual middle-class settings). Yet, the dominant image of both groups is associated with stereotypes of lower-class Blacks and Latino/as, even when they are in a middle-class socioeconomic status. This is particularly true of Black people because people of all races frequently view their relationship to blackness as a signifier of success within the United States—the further one is from blackness, the better one is perceived to be doing.[3] Thus, Black people in the United States remain, irrespective of their socioeconomic standing, symbolically at the bottom compared with other racial groups, which is illustrated in how Black women are treated in the exotic dance industry.

However, this form of symbolic racism against Black women and darker-skinned Latinas does not just function within the exotic dance industry, but also happens within marriage markets, educational institutions, real estate markets, areas of employment, health industries, and the legal system.

A recent example of Black women's low erotic capital value within the legal system appeared in the May 24, 2009 edition of the *Post-Crescent, Appleton-Fox Cities, Wisconsin* newspaper, which printed an article concerning the unsolved murders of five Black Milwaukee women, who police claim were prostitutes. The murders took place between 1986 and 2007. It was not until the week the article was released that police reveled recent DNA tests linking the murders of these women. According to the article, many people in the community felt that the women's race and the stigma of being prostitutes kept police from pursuing these crimes aggressively, and that some officers referred to prostitutes as "crack whores." All of the women who were killed were Black, except for one White woman, who police believe may have been murdered by someone else, although the suspect's DNA was found on her body. This case reveals a great deal about how erotic capital is valued and how racism and classism function to devalue the lives of people from marginalized groups, such as sex workers.

Another case of the intersection of race and erotic capital in the legal system is the 2006 case involving three White male lacrosse players from Duke University. The students were accused of raping a Black exotic dancer. Although DNA tests from the lacrosse players came back negative and they were not convicted of the rape of Crystal Gail Mangum, issues of racism, sexual violence, class inequality, and gender were prevalent in this case.

My research on racialized erotic capital among Black and Latina women in the exotic dancing industry demonstrates one example of how symbolic racism functions on an institutional level in the post-Civil Rights era. When women of color are working in predominately White clubs that offer more security and are located in areas with higher property values, they often are paid less than their White counterparts, marginalized as token hires, or employed in lower-tier job positions. Women of color working in clubs predominately employing people of color, may make good money, but are subject to unjust working conditions, customer expectations that services will be cheaper, and unsafe neighborhood spaces—erotic capital is not separate from institutions or other forms of capital.

There are institutional consequences for not being viewed as sexually desirable and/or attractive, especially for dark-skinned Black women. The low erotic capital of Black and Latina women who work in desire industries impacts their labor and immigrant rights, violence against them within and outside of their neighborhoods, ideas about community investment, and how they support their education and/or provide for their families by working in desire industries. Therefore, policymakers, immigrant rights groups, queer organizations, and feminists advocating sex workers' rights need to be aware of how women of color are positioned in this industry, and how that affects issues of fair housing policies, affordable health care, immigration policies, access to good legal advice and representation, and safe working conditions for exotic dancers. Finally, although it may be challenging, they need to finds ways to remedy the symbolic racism stratification and marginalization of women of color by implementing symbolic forms of affirmative action within clubs (i.e. making allowances for dancers experiencing symbolic racism from customers in the form of shift scheduling or promoting the shows of dancers of color more).

In the era of "colorblindness," and particularly with the historic 2009 presidential election of Barack Obama, many people in the United States believe that, as a nation, issues of race and racism no longer present the barriers they once did in the pre-Civil Rights period. However, even as the meanings of race, gender, and class shift, structural oppression is still occurring among poor and working-class people, as well as for individuals of marginal middle to upper middle class groups (people of color, White women, queer people), both symbolic representation and oppression connected with cultural stereotypes of the past mark their experiences in these new times.

Appendix

Demographics of Interviewees

Barbara, U.S. Black, late 30s
Bill, White, 38 years old
C.K., U.S. Black, 26 years old
Casey, U.S. Black and Puerto Rican, 22 years old
Cristina, Latina (Puerto Rican), 28 years old
Daniel, White, 36 years old
Denise, Latina (Dominican Republic), early 20s
Diana, Latina (Puerto Rican and German), early 20s
Edward, U.S. Black, 42 years old
Gail, U.S. Black, 26 years old
Hassen, Indian, 30 years old
Ian, Middle-Eastern, mid-30s
Jamal, U.S. Black, 28 years old
Jesse, Black, mid-30s
Joseph, White, 45 years old
Josie, Latina, mid-20s
Latrice, U.S. Black, 30 years old
Lilia, Latina (Dominican Republic), 45 years old
Mark, U.S. Black, late 30s
Melissa, Puerto Rican, early 20s
Mike, U.S. Black, 29 years old
Mona, U.S. Black and White, 26 years old
Monique, U.S. Black, early 20s
Natasha, U.S. Black, 24 years old
Nekia, U.S. Black, mid-20s
Patrick, White, 25 years old
Sheila, U.S. Black, 28 years old
Silky, U.S. Black, 39 years old
Sonya, U.S. Black, 24 years old
Spice, bi-racial U.S. Black identified, 28 years old
Tommy, Black Caribbean, mid-40s
Wanda, U.S. Black, mid-40s

Sample Research Questions

For Club Owners

What made you decide to go into this business?
What made you choose the location?
What are your criteria for hiring women?
What are the benefits to this location?
Does the neighboring market help your industry?
Do you feel you hire women of certain races? Why or why not?
Do the customers like these women? Do they ever request different types?
How do you deal with zoning issues?
How do you advertise dancers? Your business?
What business, if any, were you in before this one?
What kind of neighborhood did you grow up in?
What was the population at your school?

*For Dancers and to a Lesser Degree, Waitresses and Workers Who Are
Not Dancers*

Do you feel you make a good living working at this venue? Why or why
    not?
Is your race an asset? Why or why not?
How do customers respond to you?
How do you respond to customers of a different race?
What kind of racial/class demographic did you grow up in?
Are you currently in school?
What other jobs have you worked? What was the racial makeup?
Do you have children? If so, how has this job created conflict, if any?
What were your dating experiences like?
Do you feel you control your image?
What kinds of exchanges do you get from customers?
What other clubs have you worked in? Are they different from this one?
What are the racial demographics of your current neighborhood?

Questions for Male Customers

Why do you patronize this club?
What do you like about the dancers?
Do you feel as though you are helping dancers when you tip them?
Is there anything you wish was different about this club?
What other clubs have you gone to?

What kind of neighborhood did you grow up in? Where?
What were your dating experiences like pertaining to race/class?
Why do you attend strip clubs?
What line of work are you in?
What are your shopping experiences like?
What kind of desires do you wish to fulfill at the club?
Do you have racial preferences?
Do you feel more masculine at these clubs?

Questions for Female Customers

Do you feel conflicted seeing other women strip?
Are the dancers part of a community?
Do you see them as just there dancing?
If butch-identified, what is your relationship to femmes?
How do you view dancers?

Notes

Notes to Introduction

1. The names of the clubs are pseudonyms to protect the identity of the interviewees.

2. See the appendix for more detail regarding interview subjects.

Notes to Chapter 1

1. Timothy Gilfoyle (1992) also examines the problematic situation of gender roles for women without a male escort within the public sphere and their association with prostitution.

2. Swedish singer Jenny Lind was one of the first women to appear on stage in the 1850s, representing female moral standing as an attempt to combine art, women, and middle-class values within the theater (Allen, 1992).

3. According to Allen (1992) this form of performance also was associated with the working classes and an indicator that women performing on stage was moving from the previous association of the middle class to the lower classes with the introduction of the nude female form.

4. In the play, Menken rides a horse while wearing a pink body stocking and tunic, marking her as a subversive performer pushing the moral boundaries.

5. Allen does not indicate if the Blacks who attended the theater were all men or if women also were in attendance.

6. A waiter girl was a woman who sold alcoholic beverages in what was considered short dresses (Allen, 1991; see also Delany, 1999).

7. This is seen in the performances of comedian William Mitchell who staged burlesque shows and "delighted his mostly working-class audience with send-ups of whatever their "betters" found fashionable in literature or the theater" (Allen, 1991, p. 102).

8. There also were performances centered on blackface femininity, involving men playing lower-class wench roles, or portraying refined mulattoes who sang of romantic love (Allen, 1991). It is interesting to note the association between mixed-race femininity and sexual/romantic desire. See also Jayna Brown's *Babylon Girls: Black Women Performers and the Modern Body* (Duke University Press, 2008).

9. During this time, there also was a rise in commercial sex districts within urban areas.

10. Elizabeth Bernstein (2007) in her book, *Temporarily Yours: Intimacy, Authenticity, and the Commerce of Sex,* argues that during this period many sexual services were available for purchase in urban centers, especially for bourgeois men. She avers that these services included "diverse forms of prostitution as well as erotic masked balls, private modeling shows, and pornography" (p. 171).

11. The Ziegfeld Follies were a series of theatrical productions that ran on Broadway in New York from 1907 to 1931 and were inspired by Folies Bergères of Paris (Allen, 1992).

12. According to Allen, during economic hardship, "high-class" venues find it harder to attract audiences because of high admission rates; vis-à-vis "lower-class" forms of entertainment. This was the case with burlesque during the Depression. The Minsky brothers of New York named the art "striptease" and featured performer Gypsy Rose Lee, who helped popularize burlesque during this time (Frank, 2002; see also Friedman, 2000).

13. The image of strip clubs as seedy is illustrated in the 2007 film, *Planet Terror*, produced and written by Robert Rodriguez.

Notes to Chapter 2

1. Information is from the 2004 U.S. Census Bureau.

2. Jill Jonnes makes a distinction in her book, *South Bronx Rising* about the various types of Jewish people who moved to New York during this time. According to Jonnes, the German Jews had a longer history of being established in New York than did Russian and Polish Jews, were horrified at the conditions and poverty of the eastern European Jews, and felt culturally obligated to help them out economically (Jonnes, 2002).

3. Jonnes acknowledges that Blacks have always been in New York, from the time of slavery and the Harlem Renaissance, but now in larger numbers.

4. White U.S. veterans were able to take advantage of the GI Bill and enrolled in the CUNY system, and moved to predominately White suburbs, thus taking resources with them.

5. See Ruth Frankenberg (1993) for more on race and social geography.

6. In the 1996 documentary, *Hookers at the Point* by Brent Owens, this aspect of street prostitution in the South Bronx is explored. See also Kevin Mumford (1997).

7. See also cultural anthropologist, Katherine Frank (2002), who discusses the role of club ranking in Laurelton by customers, and racial geography:

> Though not explicitly stated, there seemed to be an implicit assumption among the customers that an upscale club was also primarily white. Strip clubs are frequently spoken of in Laurelton as being black or white, as are sections of town and other places of business. . . . White clubs remained unmarked; that is their whiteness was not offered in a description unless race was already being discussed. (p. 57)

8. For a further discussion of this topic, see Frank (2002). In my research I learned that single women are prohibited from entering Temptations without a man because some dancers fear competition from female customers.

9. A tip-out is a fee dancers often pay management after a shift; sometimes they also give a percentage of their tips to the DJ.

10. The relationship between lesbianism and stripping has been documented by many scholars (Barton, 2006; Frank, 2002).

11. See Phillip Bourgois (2003) for his reference to inverted patriarchy among women in Spanish Harlem and for more on this topic regarding how women navigate the male-dominated crack industry of Spanish Harlem.

12. This is especially true for men (and women) who may be undocumented immigrants in fear of being deported.

13. It is worth noting that although the men are encouraged to eat, the dancers are expected to maintain a lean body and control their food intake.

14. The *New York Post* is a newspaper geared more toward the working class.

15. When observing these men passing out flyers, I asked them how much they made.

16. The notion of body and form also can be applied to the dancer's body and form; women's bodies at Temptations may be curvier than women at Conquest, whose bodies are more lean and thin with the exception of women who are busty or who may have had breast implants. Slim bodies are associated with the middle class, whereas curvier/overweight bodies are associated with the working class.

Notes to Chapter 3

1. Notions of intimacy also are exchanged between dancers and customers. See Elizabeth Bernstein (2007).

2. The EBT card (Electronic Benefit Transfer) has replaced the paper version of food stamps. The card also marks the class difference between this woman and many of the dancers and customers at Conquest.

3. In his study of interracial prostitution during the 1920s Kevin Mumford (1997) notes that many White men perceived Black prostitutes as aggressive and thus more immoral than their White counterparts.

4. This view is underscored by Patricia Hill Collins, who argues that stereotypes of "unnaturally strong Black women" and "weak Black men" contribute to gender tension among Black men and women, wherein Black women's accomplishments are seen as holding back racial progress. Collins (2004) avers that:

> Within this logic, African American progress also requires weakening "unnaturally strong Black women . . . Black women are told that their assertiveness is holding African Americans back, especially men. (p. 183)

5. Other dancers I interviewed confirmed Edward's opinions of customers wanting more services for less money at Black clubs, and the exchanges between dancers and customers.

6. Bourdieu (1991) examines the role of legitimate language and power relations in *Language and Symbolic Power* when he states that:

> It is necessary to distinguish between the capital necessary for the simple production of more or less legitimate ordinary speech, on the one hand, and the capital of instruments of expression which is needed to produce a written discourse worthy of being published, that is to say, made official, on the other. This production of instruments of production, such as rhetorical devices, genres, legitimate styles and manners and, more generally, all the formulations destined to be "authoritative" and to be cited as examples of "good usage," confers on those who engage in it as a power over language and thereby over the ordinary users of language, as well as over their capital. (p. 58)

7. Collins uses this term when referring to Black feminist thought designed to empower Black women to resist dominant ideology aimed at oppressing them based on race, class, gender, and sexuality.

Notes to Chapter 4

1. See the work of Stryker and Van Buskirk (1996) for more information on queer history in the Bay Area.

2. I define gender variant and gender nonconforming as expressions of gender where individuals dress in a manner not consistent with their sex.

3. Silky also promotes "Pimps up, Hos down," an event that takes place every third Saturday in Oakland and is promoted by Butchlicious. It is an event in which women dress up either like a pimp or a prostitute; usually the femme is the ho, and the butch/aggressive is the pimp. Silky, as the promoter, also dresses up as a pimp.

4. An *aggressive* is a masculine-identified woman like the category of butch; *aggressive* is the contemporary term among younger masculine-identified women. Also see the April 2007 issue of the *Village Voice* on gender roles and aggressive-identified women, and the film *The Aggressives*.

5. In recent years, Oakland has experienced a surge of crime and violent events. A few weeks before I arrived in Oakland, a Black woman was set on fire (and survived) in an elementary school near Piedmont.

6. This practice also exists in some Black heterosexual spaces, especially in poor/working-class neighborhoods, where a dress code is enforced, along with people being frisked for weapons.

7. Baby Phat is an urban clothing line for women, started in 1998 by Kimora Lee Simmons.

8. Although I am describing the gender binary of butch and femme dynamics of the space, I don't want this description to be read as normalizing heterosexual roles where butch/femme identities are viewed as copies of heterosexual roles. I agree with Judith Butler (2004) that "categories of butch and femme were not copies of a more originary heterosexuality, but they showed how the so-called originals, men

and women within the heterosexual frame similarly constructed" (p. 209). See also Kennedy and Davis (1993).

9. This form of exchange reflects what Paul Cressey (1932) observed in the taxi-dance halls among dancers and customers, except that the dancers were White and often took advantage of the Asian male customers' search for acceptance within U.S. society and culture, viewing their interactions with White dancers as a way to assimilate.

10. Sandy also stated that she made about $200 to $250 dancing, which is $100 less than what Spice said she made.

11. More on racial marketing is examined in the following chapter on marketing and Web sites of clubs.

12. Grills is slang for gold teeth, which is associated with the South, and considered low-brow, but has now become part of hip-hop culture

13. I asked Spice how she knew dancers were not making much money on stage for graphic shows, when it is sometimes hard to see the money audience members give dancers on stage. She said the wad of money often is smaller compared with when she performs.

14. Mary Patillo-McCoy (1998), in her article "Church Culture as Strategy of Action in the Black Community," discusses the multiple functions that the Black church serves in many Black communities as an institution:

> The church acts simultaneously as a school, a bank, a benevolent society, a political organization, a party hall, and a spiritual base. As one of the few institutions owned and operated by African Americans the church is often the center of activity in black communities. (p. 769)

15. East Bay Church of Religious Science also is in Oakland. It is a popular church attended by many in the East Bay Black community, including those who are LGBT and sex workers.

16. In *Passing By: Gender and Public Harassment,* Carol Brooks Gardner (1995) observes that a strategy some women used to deal with or ward off sexual harassment is role reversal or a type of "turnabout" where women reverse the gender roles with their (male) harassers:

> Some women noted that they practiced a trick or turnabout (role reversal) on the harasser. In these situations the women elaborately affected to be doing something other than what she was doing or reversed roles with the man, with the woman becoming the pincher or stalker, for example. (p. 216)

Therefore, it can be argued that the behavior of some female customers at Girlielicious could be a result of trying to navigate male space or an internalization of the behavior of some men they have observed in public spaces.

17. The 2003 death of Sakia Gunn at a bus stop in Newark, New Jersey brought issues of race, class, and gender identity to the forefront, While at the bus stop, a Black man approached Sakia and her friends, and stabbed her to death after

she said she was a lesbian. Many believe she was murdered because she challenged traditional gender roles and male authority as a self-identified aggressive.

18. In summer 1996, the Lusty Lady made history as the only strip club in the country to successfully unionize.

19. In earlier research I note that for many working-class women of color and White women, the opportunity to make more money is a deciding factor in whether or not they choose a club like the Lusty Lady with a set wage per hour and no opportunity for tips. Spice would make anywhere from $50 to $1,000 per shift.

20. I contacted Sandy the day after to ask about the details of the fight.

Notes to Chapter 5

1. *Bling* is a term used within the hip-hop community to express a lifestyle built around notions of conspicuous consumption, such as wearing expensive jewelry and other accoutrements, excessive spending, and ostentation of wealth.

2. If one were to click on the party services link a photo of three White women (one blonde, the other two brunettes) and a White man appears. The women are caressing and kissing the man. It is interesting that this is the image representing the experience one could have at a club that is mostly Black and Latino in terms of workers.

3. Katherine Frank (2002) does note that this middle space where lesbianism can exist also could be a venue in which the dancer can express her own desires.

4. The names of the dancers also point to status and class because some are associated with White bourgeois culture.

5. I note that "champagne" is misspelled on the Web site and that "high-end" should be hyphenated, which indicates the class and education status of the management and many of the people who work at and patronize Temptations.

6. Unlike the Web site for Temptations, Conquest's Web site has sound affects, indicating a higher budget used for advertising. The site also shows the corporate earnings of the club and its value in the stock market.

7. Conquest has stock options, which indicates a level of prestige and privilege compared with a club like Temptations.

8. MySpace is a virtual community where people make friends, browse users' profiles, and advertise their art.

9. I am assuming management of the club created this page.

10. See Celine Parrenas Shimizu (2007) for more about Asian women and controlling images in the media.

11. See Sarah Barnet-Weiser (1999). She observes the notion of citizenship, pluralism, and racial inclusion in beauty pageants in the United States:

> The Miss America pageant produces images and narratives that articulate dominate expectations about who and what "American" women are (and should be) at the same time as it narrates who and what the nation itself should be through promises of citizenship, fantasies of agency, and tolerant pluralism. (p. 159)

12. Some flyers have some words in Black English, underscoring the race and class of the target audience for the event.

13. A blog is a section on a person's Web site where commentaries and opinions are posted.

14. This Internet posting connecting issues of Black male violence and the sex industry brings to mind the 2006 murder of Sean Bell, who was murdered by police in Queens, New York at a bachelor party outside of a strip club that was known to be the site of frequent police raids.

15. Spice's posting regarding explicit shows also speaks to the economic condition and low erotic value of dancers who perform these shows in hopes of making extra money.

Notes to Chapter 6

1. For further reading about skin tone stratification in the workplace see Goldsmith, Hamilton, and Darity (2007); see also Glenn (2009) and Hunter (2002).

2. Later in my stay, I witnessed some White customers to whom she tried to sell massages buy them from White dancers. It was very busy that night, so I didn't get a chance to ask these customers why they didn't buy a massage from her, so I rely on participant-observation to analyze my data.

3. Similarly, Sarah Weiser-Barnet (1999) argued in her book, *The Most Beautiful Girl in the World,* that beauty pageants are a way that women perform notions of respectability, national identity, democracy, and citizenship.

4. I did not encounter any dancers who had plastic surgery, but at Temptations I was told by various dancers that women had surgery done, especially breast implants, and that this was common with the transgendered women who worked there. I did not meet any of these women during my fieldwork, but note that I did not hear of Conquest hiring transgendered women, at least not in my fieldwork. See Wendy Chapkis' (1986) work for more on women and appearances.

5. In *Global Sex Workers: Rights, Resistance, and Redefinition,* Kamala Kempadoo and Jo Doezema (1998) assert that with growing numbers of jobs being outsourced and the gendered impact of globalization, along with state funds such as welfare decreasing, the number of women working in the service sector had increased, especially within the sex industry. So, for women like Denise, work in service jobs, such as the sex industry, is an extension of service labor jobs.

6. In the article, "Gender, Race, and Urban Policing: The Experience of African-American Youths" Rod K. Brunson and Jody Miller (2006), when examining underpolicing in inner-city communities, quote criminologist David A. Klinger, stating:

> The police are less responsive in poor urban neighborhoods because they believe that certain crimes are normative in these communities and they view victims in such contexts as deserving. (p. 534)

7. This is not an uncommon sight in many inner-city places of businesses (such as the post office, liquor stores, check-cashing venues), which reinforces the police state of many low-income communities of color.

Notes to Chapter 7

1. See Conley (1999) for a further discussion of the wealth gap among Blacks and Whites, even as Black may have a higher earning power.

2. Although the Black and Latino/a middle classs have increased, members of this group remain unstable compared with Whites. For further information see the Wheary, Shapiro, Draut, and Meschede (2008), "Economic (In)Security: The Experience of the African-American and Latino Middle Classes," published by the Institute on Assets and Social Policy.

3. See Twine and Warren (1997). In this article the authors argue that contrary to the idea that Whites are becoming a fast minority, especially in states such as California, the expansion of whiteness as category can incorporate certain Asian Americans and Latinos/as at the expense of Black exclusion. See also Virginia Dominquez's (1986) work on whiteness and racialization.

References

Allen, R. (1991). *Horrible prettiness: Burlesque and American culture*. Chapel Hill: The University of North Carolina Press.

Barry, K. (1984). *Female sexual slavery*. New York: NYU Press.

Barton, B. (2006). *Stripped: Inside the lives of exotic dancers*. New York: NYU Press.

Bederman G. (1994). *Manliness and civilization: A cultural history of gender and race in the United States, 1880–1917*. Chicago: Chicago University Press.

Benson, S. (1987). *Counter cultures: Saleswomen, managers, and customers in American department stores, 1890–1940*. Chicago: University of Illinois Press.

Bernstein, E. (2007). *Temporarily yours: Intimacy, authenticity, and the commerce of sex*. Chicago: University of Chicago Press.

Bernstein, E., & Schaffer, L. (2004). *Regulating sex: The politics of intimacy and identity*. New York: Routledge.

Bordo, S. (1993). *Unbearable weight: Feminism, Western culture, and the body*. Berkeley: University of California Press.

Bourdieu, P. (1991). *Language and symbolic power*. Cambridge, MA: Harvard University Press.

Bourdieu, P. (2001). *Masculine domination*. Stanford, CA: Stanford University Press.

Bourdieu, P. (2002). *Distinction: A social critique of the judgement of taste*. Cambridge, MA: Harvard University Press.

Bourgois, P. (2003). *In search of respect: Selling crack in El Barrio*. Cambridge: Cambridge University Press.

Bradley-Engen, M. (2009). *Naked lives: Inside the world of exotic dance*. Albany: State University of New York Press.

Brooks, S. (1997, January). Organizing from behind the glass: Exotic dancers ready to unionize. *Z Magazine*, pp. 11–14.

Brown, Jayna. (2008). *Babylon Girls: Black Women Performers and the Modern Body*. Durham, NC: Duke University Press.

Brunson, K. R., & Miller, J. (2006). Gender, race, and urban policing: The experience of African-American youths. *Gender and Society, 20*(4), 531–552.

Butler, J. (1990). *Gender trouble: Feminism and the subversion of identity*. New York: Routledge.

Butler, J. (2004). *Undoing gender*. New York: Routledge.

Cabeza, A. L. (2004). Between money and love: Sex, tourism, and citizenship in Cuba and the Dominican Republic. *SIGNS: Journal of Women and Society,* *29*(4), 986–1015.

Castells, M. (1977). *The urban question: A Marxist approach* (A. Sheridan, Trans.). London: Edward Arnold; Cambridge, MA: MIT Press.

Chang, G. (2002). *Disposable domestics: Immigrant women workers in the global economy.* Boston: South End Press.

Chapkis, W. (1986). *Beauty secrets: Women and the politics of appearance.* Boston: South End Press.

Chapkis, W. (1996). *Live sex acts: Women performing erotic labor.* New York: Routledge.

Chauncey, G. (1995). *Gay New York: Gender, urban culture, and the making of the gay male world, 1890–1940.* New York: Basic Books.

Collins, P. H. (1990). *Black feminist thought.* New York: Routledge.

Collins, P. H. (2004). *Black sexual politics: African Americans, gender, and the new racism.* New York: Routledge.

Conley, D. (1999). *Being black, living in the red: Race, wealth, and social policy in America.* Berkeley: University of California Press.

Cressey, P. (1932). *The taxi-dance hall: A sociological study on commercialized recreation and city life.* Chicago: University of Chicago Press.

Crenshaw, K. W. (1995). Mapping the margins: Intersectionality, identity politics, and violence against women of color. In K. Crenshaw, N. Gotanda, G. Peller, & K. Thomas (Eds.), *Critical race theory: The key writings that formed the movement* (pp. 357–383). New York: The New Press.

Delacoste, F., & Alexander, P. (1987). *Sex work: Writings by women in the sex industry.* San Francisco: Cleis Press.

Delany, S. (1999). *Times Square Red, Times Square Blue.* New York: NYU Press.

Dominquez, V. (1986). *White by definition: Social classification in Creole Louisiana.* New Brunswick, NJ: Rutgers University Press.

Drake, St. C., & Cayton, H. (1945). *Black metropolis: A study of negro life in a northern city.* New York: HarperTorch Books.

Dworkin, A. (1981). *Pornography: Men possessing women.* New York: Perigee Books.

Erenberg, L. (1981). *Stepping out: New York nightlife and the transformation of American culture, 1890–1930.* Westport, CT: Greenwood Press.

Faderman, L. (1932). *Odd girls and twilight lovers: A history of lesbian life in twentieth-century America.* New York: Penguin.

Foucault, M. (1975). *Discipline and punish: The birth of the prison.* New York: Vintage.

Foucault, M. (1978). *The history of sexuality: An introduction* (Vol. 1). New York: Vintage.

Frank, K. (2002). *G-strings and sympathy: Strip club regulars and male desire.* Durham, NC: Duke University Press.

Frankenberg, R. (1993). *White women, race matters: The social construction of whiteness.* Minneapolis: University of Minnesota Press.

Frazier, E. F. (1957). *Black bourgeoisie: The rise of a new middle class in the United States.* New York: The Free Press.

Friedman, A. (2000). *Prurient interests: Gender, democracy, and obscenity in New York City 1909–1945.* New York: Columbia University Press.

Gardner, C. B. (1995). *Passing by: Sexual harassment and public space.* Berkeley: University of California Press.

Gilfoyle T. (1992). *City of eros: New York City prostitution, and the commericalization of sex, 1790–1920.* New York: Norton.

Girshick, L. (2002). *Woman-to-woman sexual violence: Does she call it rape?* Philadelphia: Temple University Press.

Glenn, E. N. (2002). *Unequal freedom: How race and gender shaped American citizenship and labor.* Cambridge, MA: Harvard University Press.

Glenn, E. N. (2009). *Shades of difference: Why skin color matters.* Stanford, CA: Stanford University Press.

Goldsmith, A., Hamilton, D., & Darity, W. Jr. (2007). From dark to light: Skin color and wages among African Americans. *Journal of Human Resources, 42*(4), 701–738.

Green, A. I. (2005). The social organization of desire: The sexual fields approach. *Sociological Theory, 26,* 25–50.

Haidarali, L. (2005). Polishing brown diamonds: African American women, popular magazines, and the advent of modeling in early postwar America. *Journal of Women's History, 17,* 1.

Haiken E. (1999). *Venus envy: A history of cosmetic surgery.* Baltimore: Johns Hopkins University Press.

Halberstam, J. (1998). *Female masculinity.* Durham, NC: Duke University Press.

Hanna, J. (1998). Undressing the First Amendment and corsetting the striptease dancer. *Drama Review, 42,* 38–69.

Hunter, M. (2002). "If you're light you're alright": Light skin as social capital for women of color. *Gender and Society, 16*(2).

Jacobs, J. (1965). *Death and life of great American cities.* New York: Random House.

Jacobson, M. F. (1998). *Whiteness of a different color: European immigrants and the alchemy of race.* Cambridge, MA: Harvard University Press.

Jarrett, L. (1997). *Stripping in time: A history of exotic dancing.* London: Rivers Oram Press.

Jenkins, R. (2002). *Pierre Bourdieu.* New York: Routledge.

Jonnes, J. (2002). *South Bronx rising.* New York: Fordham University Press.

Kempadoo K., & Dozema, J. (1998). *Global sex workers.* New York: Routledge.

Kennedy, E. L., & Davis, M. D. (1994). *Boots of leather, slippers of gold: The history of lesbian community.* New York: Penguin Books.

Kolko, B., Nakamura, L., & Rodmann, G. (2000). *Race in cyberspace.* New York: Routledge.

Kornblum, W. (1974). *Blue collar community.* Chicago: University of Chicago Press.

Lacy, K. (2007). *Blue-chip black: Race, class, and status in the new black middle class.* Berkeley: University of California Press.

Lorde, A. (1984). *Sister outsider.* Berkeley, CA: The Crossing Press.

MacKinnon, C. A. (1989). *Toward a feminist theory of the state.* Cambridge, MA: Harvard University Press.

Massey, D., & Denton, N. (1993). *American apartheid: Segregation and the making of the underclass.* Cambridge, MA: Harvard University Press.

McClintock, A. (1995). *Imperial leather: Race, gender, and sexuality in the colonial contest.* New York: Routledge.

Miller-Young, M. (2007). *Hip-Hop Honeys and Da Hustlaz: Black Sexualities in the New Hip-Hop Pornography.* Meridians: feminism, race, transnationalism—Volume 8, Number 1, pp. 261–292.

Moore, M. R. (2006). Lipstick or Timberlands? Meanings of gender presentation in black lesbian communities. *SIGNS: Journal of Women in Culture and Society, 32*(1), 113–139.

Mumford, K. (1997). *Interzones: Black and white sex districts in Chicago and New York in the early twentieth century.* New York: Columbia University Press.

Nagle, J. (1997). *Whores and other feminists.* New York: Routledge.

Nagel J. (2003). *Race, ethnicity, and sexuality: Intimate intersections, forbidden frontiers.* New York: Oxford University Press.

Owens, B. (2002). *Hookers at the point.* Mti Home Video.

Park, R. (1950). *Race and culture.* New York: The Free Press.

Park, R., Burgess, E., & McKenzie, R. D. (1925). *The city.* Chicago: University of Chicago Press.

Patillo-McCoy, M. (1998). Church culture as strategy of action in the black community. *American Sociological Review, 63,* 767–784.

Pattillo-McCoy, M. (2000). *Black picket fences: Privilege and peril among the Black middle-class.* Chicago: University of Chicago Press.

Puar, J.K. (2001). Global circuits: Transnational sexualities and Trinidad. *SIGNS: Journal of Women and Society. 26*(4), 1039–65.

Quadagno, J. (1996). *The color of welfare: How racism undermined the war on poverty.* New York: Oxford University Press.

Reskin, B. (1990). *Job queues, gender queues: Explaining women's inroads into male occupations.* Philadelphia: Temple University Press.

Roberts, D. (1997). *Killing the black body: Race, reproduction, and the meaning of liberty.* New York: Pantheon.

Roediger, D. (1999). *Wages of whiteness: Race and the making of the American working-class.* New York: Verso.

Romero, M. (2002). *Maid in the U.S.A.* New York: Routledge.

Rupp, L., & Taylor, V. (2003). *Drag queens at the 801 Cabaret.* Chicago: University of Chicago Press.

Rydell, R. W. (1984). *All the world's a fair: Visions of empire at American international expositions, 1876–1916.* Chicago: University of Chicago Press.

Scherer, A. G., & Palazzo, G. (2008). *Handbook of research on global corporate citizenship.* Northampton, MA: Edward Elgar Publishing.

Shimizu, P. C. (2007). *The hypersexuality of race: Performing Asian/American women on screen and scene.* Durham, NC: Duke University Press.

Spain, D. (1992). *Gendered spaces.* Chapel Hill: University of North Carolina Press.

Stein, A. (1997). *Sex and sensibility: Stories of a lesbian generation.* Berkeley: University of California Press.

Stryker S., & Van Buskirk, J. (1996). *Gay by the bay: A history of queer culture in the San Francisco Bay.* San Francisco: Chronicle Books.

Sternlieb, G., & Beaton, W. P. (1972). *The zone of emergence: A case study of Plainfield, New Jersey.* New Brunswick, NJ: Transaction Books.

Twine, F. W. (1997). *Racism in a racial democracy: The maintenance of white supremacy in Brazil.* New Brunswick and London: Rutgers University Press.

Twine, F. W., & Warren, J. (1997). White Americans, the new minority? Non-blacks and the ever-expanding boundaries of whiteness. *Journal of Black Studies, 28*(2).

Waldinger R. (1996). *Still the promised city: African-Americans and new immigrants in postindustrial New York.* Cambridge, MA: Harvard University Press.

Wallace, R. (1990). Urban desertification, public health and public order: "Planned shrinkage," violent death, substance abuse and AIDS in the Bronx. *Social Science and Medicine, 31*(7), 801–813.

Weber, M. (1958). *From Max Weber.* New York: Oxford University Press.

Weiser-Barnet S. (1999). *The most beautiful girl in the world: Beauty pageants and national identity.* Berkeley: University of California Press.

Wheary, J., Shapiro, T. M., Draut, T., & Meschede, T. (2008). *Economic (in)security: The experience of the African-American and Latino middle classes.* Waltham, MA: Institute on Assets and Social Policy.

Williams, C. (2006). *Inside toyland: Working, shopping, and social inequality.* Berkeley: University of California Press.

Williams, T. (1992). *Crack house: Notes from the end of the line.* Reading, MA: Addison-Wesley.

Wilson, W. J. (1978). *The declining significance of race: Blacks and changing American institutions.* Chicago: University of Chicago Press.

Zanger, J. (1974). The minstrel show as theater of misrule. *Quarterly Journal of Speech, 60*, 33–38.

Index

advertising, 21, 33–34, 50, 51
  in Brazil, 75
  symbolic violence in, 73–75
  See also Web sites
agency
  empowerment through, 5, 110n7
  power relations and, 47–48, 57–58
AIDS, 18
Allen, Robert C., 11–17
American Indians. *See* Native Americans
assimilation, cultural, 91–94
Astor Place Theater, 12, 14
Atlanta, 40
"attractiveness," 82
  beauty pageants and, 112n11
  hiring practices and, 28–29, 58–59,
    68, 91, 99–102
  See also erotic capital

bachelor parties, 74, 78
Bailey, Stephanie, 3
ballet, 12–13
Barnet-Weiser, Sarah, 112n11
beauty pageants, 112n11, 113n3
Bell, Sean, 113n14
belly dancing, 15–16
Bernstein, Elizabeth, 108n10
bisexuality, 49, 56, 72
"bling," 72, 112n1
blogs, 84
  See also Web sites
Bordo, Susan, 56
Bourdieu, Pierre, 6
  on field, 37

  on habitus, 37
  on language, 110n6
  on meals, 34–35
Bourgois, Phillipe, 109n11
Bowery Theater, 12, 14
Brazil, colorism in, 75
breast implants, 29, 73, 92, 109n16,
  113n4
Breyer, Johanna, 1
Broadway Theater, 12
Brunson, Rod K., 113n6
burlesque, 11–13
  audience for, 14, 17
  liquor licenses and, 17
  racial stratification in, 15
  transformation of, 15–17
Butler, Judith, 53, 63–64

cabarets, 14, 16, 34
  licensing of, 17
Cast Off Your Old Tired Ethics
  (COYOTE), 1
Chauncey, George, 30
citizenship, 91–94, 97
class stratification, 24–25, 33–35
  burlesque versus cabarets, 17
  clothing and, 26
  theater-going public and, 13–14
Clinton, Bill, 6, 100
clothing, 50–51
  of customers, 26, 28, 41, 55, 61, 64
  of strippers, 26, 58, 61
Collins, Patricia Hill, 47, 87–88, 109n4
colonialism, race and, 15–16

colorism, 2, 4, 32, 60, 102
  in Brazil, 75
  labor stratification and, 87–91, 95, 97
  on Web sites, 71, 74–76, 79
  See also race
concert saloons, 14
Conquest club (Manhattan), 7, 29–35
  cover charges at, 29, 31
  cultural capital at, 34–35
  dancers of color at, 11
  food menu at, 35
  location of, 31
  racial stratification at, 88–91
  social networking at, 39–40
  Temptations Cabaret versus, 29–31, 41
  Web site of, 9, 77–81, 112n6
"cooch" dance, 15–16
cosmetic surgery, 92
  See also breast implants
cover charges, 8
  at Conquest, 29, 31, 88
  at Temptations Cabaret, 25
COYOTE (Cast Off Your Old Tired Ethics), 1
Cressy, Paul, 5–6, 111n9
cultural capital, 34–35, 37
  erotic capital and, 45–48, 57–58
  language skills and, 46–47, 110n6, 112n5

Delany, Samuel, 18, 19
Denton, Nancy, 23
desire industries
  in Chicago, 5–6
  criminalization of, 18–19
  history of, 5–6, 11–19
  labor stratification in, 87–94
  in New York, 6, 11–19, 27
  same-sex, 49–69
  zoning laws and, 27
  See also erotic capital
Doezema, Jo, 113n5
Dominicans immigrants, 75, 93
dress code, for customers, 26, 28, 55, 110n6
  See also clothing

drug use, 23, 61, 65
  prostitution and, 25, 45–46
  at strip clubs, 18
Duke University's Lacrosse team scandal, 101

Electronic Benefit Transfer (EBT) card, 38, 109n2
entry fees. *See* cover charges
erotic capital, 6–7, 37, 82
  class and, 35
  community and, 51–53, 83–85, 96
  cultural capital for, 45–48, 57–58
  exchanges with, 40–45, 56–59
  hiring practices and, 28–29, 58–59, 68, 91, 99–102
  marketing of, 26, 59–60
  performance of, 53–54, 59, 61–62
  undervaluing of, 40–45, 61–62, 76, 91, 95, 99–102, 109n5
  violence and, 66–69, 73–75
  See also desire industries
eugenics movement, 15
Exotic Dancer's Alliance, 1, 3

Follies Bergères, 108n11
food menus, 33–35
food stamps, 38, 109n2
Forrest, Edwin, 14
Foucault, Michel, 63, 94
Frankenberg, Ruth, 108n5
Frank, Katherine, 16, 17, 108n7, 112n3
freak shows, 16
Friedman, Andrea, 14, 17

gangsta rap. *See* rap music
Gardner, Carol Brooks, 111n16
gay urban culture, 18, 30, 49
  See also lesbians
gender issues
  clothing styles and, 50–51
  club managers and, 58–59
  role identity and, 54–56, 63–66, 68, 82, 110n4
  stratification and, 5–6
  women in strip clubs and, 25, 27, 109n8

Gilfoyle, Tim, 14, 107n1
Girlielicious club (Oakland, CA), 7, 8,
    49–69
    advertising by, 50, 51
    Web site of, 9, 85
Giuliani, Rudy, 8, 18, 27, 31
gold digging, 37, 44–45
gold teeth, 55, 61, 111n12
Green, Adam, 6–7
Greenwich Village, 30, 31
    See also New York City
Gunn, Sakia, 111n17

habitus, 37, 38
Hanna, Judith, 18
harassment
    police, 4, 38, 51–52, 97, 113n14
    sexual, 4, 51, 52, 59, 111n16
Harlem, 22, 50, 52
hip-hop clothing styles, 28, 41, 55, 61,
    64
hip-hop music, 4, 32, 51, 68
    See also rap music
hiring practices, 28–29, 58–59, 68, 91,
    99–102
HIV disease, 18
home-schooling, 57
hypersexualization, of women of color,
    39–42, 45, 52, 95, 99

immigrants, 22, 91–94, 97, 100–102,
    108n2
Internet. See Web sites
"inverted patriarchy" (Bourgois), 28,
    109n11
Italian immigrants, 22

Jackson, Andrew, 14
Jacobs, Jane, 18–19
Jewish immigrants, 22, 92, 108n2
Jonnes, Jill, 22–23

Kempadoo, Kamala, 113n5
Klinger, David A., 113n6

labor stratification, 87–91, 95
    among immigrants, 91–94, 97

language
    Bourdieu on, 110n6
    cultural capital and, 46–47, 112n5
lap dances, 26, 40, 61, 76
Lee, Gypsy Rose, 108n12
lesbians, 100
    bisexuals and, 49, 56, 72
    male gaze and, 72–73
    in strip clubs, 25, 49–69, 109n10
    Web sites for, 81–83
    See also gay urban culture
lighting, at strip clubs, 26
Lind, Jenny, 107n2
living pictures, 13
Lusty Lady Theater (San Francisco),
    1–2, 67, 112n18

Macready, William Charles, 14
male strippers, 4
Mangum, Crystal Gail, 101
massages, 38, 113n2
Massey, Doug, 23
McClintock, Anne, 15, 97
melodrama, 12
Menken, Adah, 13, 107n4
methodology, 7–8, 104–105
Miller, Jody, 113n6
Minsky brothers, 108n12
minstrel shows, 15, 16, 107n8
Mitchell Brother's Theater, 18, 67
Mitchell, William, 107n7
Moore, Mignon, 50
mothers, single, 6, 44, 59
Mumford, Kevin J., 6, 109n3
music
    club ambience and, 26, 42, 54, 88
    hip-hop, 4, 32, 51, 68
    musicals, 13
    rap, 4, 42, 60, 64, 99

Nagel, Joane, 87
naming practices, 112n4
National Public Radio (NPR), 99–100
Native Americans, 15, 16, 22
networking, 39–40, 57–58
New York City
    demographics of, 21, 30

New York City *(continued)*
  gangs of, 23
  Greenwich Village in, 30, 31
  history of, 11–19, 22–23
  Puerto Ricans in, 22–23
  residential segregation in, 23, 30
  See also specific venues, e.g., Temptations Cabaret

Obama, Barack, 102
oil wrestling, 72
Owens, Brent, 108n6

Park, Robert, 91–92
Passar, Dawn, 1
passing, racial, 5, 60, 79, 90
Patillo-McCoy, Mary, 111n14
patriarchy, "inverted," 28, 109n11
Planet Terror (film), 108n13
Playboy Magazine, 17
police harassment, 4, 38, 51–52, 97, 113n14
pornography, 5
  Black women in, 51
  health ordinances and, 18
poverty, racialized, 23
power relations, 47–48, 63
prostitution, 18, 25
  coerced, 4
  drug use and, 25, 45–46
  interracial, 6, 109n3
  Mumford on, 6, 109n3
  murders related to, 101
  race and, 16, 91
  in theaters, 12, 14
Puerto Ricans, in New York City, 22–23
Puritans, 12

questionnaires, 104–105

race, 4–6, 29–30, 34
  colonialism and, 15–16
  crossing boundaries of, 5, 38–39, 41–45, 59–60, 79, 90
  gender roles and, 64–66
  gold digging and, 37, 44–45

poverty and, 23
prostitution and, 16, 91
  See also colorism
rap music, 4, 42, 60, 64, 99
  See also music
religiosity, 62–63, 111n14
Rodriguez, Robert, 108n13
Roosevelt, Franklin, 22
Rupp, Leila, 53
Russian immigrants, 39, 89, 92, 93, 108n2

segregation, 5, 100
  New York neighborhoods and, 23, 30
  Oakland neighborhoods and, 51–52
  in theaters, 14
Service Employee International Union (SEIU) Local 790, 1, 3
sex clubs, 42–43
sexual harassment, 4, 51, 52, 59, 111n16
Shimizu, Celine Parrenas, 112n10
Simmons, Kimora Lee, 110n7
slavery, 14, 87
social networking, 39–40, 57–58
stage fees, 4, 18, 59, 62, 87
status. *See* class stratification
stereotyping, 4, 82, 100–101
  of gold diggers, 37, 44–45
  in minstrel shows, 15
  of strong Black women, 109n4
symbolic capital, 37

tableaux vivants, 13
taxi-dance halls, 5–6, 111n9
Taylor, Verta, 53
Temptations Cabaret (Bronx), 7, 21–31
  advertising by, 21, 33–34
  Conquest club versus, 29–31, 41
  cover charge for, 25
  erotic capital at, 25–30, 35, 37
  food menu at, 33–34
  location of, 22–24
  racial stratification at, 88
  Web site of, 9, 34, 71–72, 75–77, 79, 85

Thompson, Lydia, 11, 13
"tip-out," 28, 109n9
tipping, 18, 40–41, 44, 61–62, 78, 93,
    95, 97
transgendered people, 49–50, 55, 61,
    63, 113n4
Twine, F. W., 75, 114n4

undervaluing, of erotic capital, 40–45,
    61–62, 76, 91, 95, 99–102,
    109n5
unionization drives, 1, 3–4, 112n18

vaudeville shows, 14
Victorian theater, 12
videotaping, by customers, 3
violence, 52, 54–55, 84, 95–97, 111n17
    negotiating of, 66–69
    police, 38, 51–52, 113n14
    relational, 64–66
    symbolic, 73–75

waitresses, 27, 38, 40, 79, 93, 104
Wallace, Roderick, 23

Warren, J., 75, 114n4
Weber, Max, 52
Web site(s), 71–85
    blogs and, 84
    of Conquest club, 9, 77–81, 112n6
    of Girlielicious, 85
    for lesbians, 81–83
    of Temptations Cabaret, 9, 34,
        71–72, 75–77, 79, 85
Weiser-Barnet, Sarah, 113n3
women
    "aggressive," 38–39, 44–45, 109n3
    hypersexualization of, 39–42, 45, 52,
        95, 99
    unaccompanied, 25, 27, 109n8
    violent, 64–69
    See also gender
World's Columbian Exposition (1893),
    15
wrestling, 72

Zanger, Jules, 15
Ziegfeld Follies, 17, 108n11
zoning laws, 18–19, 27, 31, 33

65823063R00083

Made in the USA
Middletown, DE
04 March 2018